AF560837

Image and Culture

The Dynamics of Literary, Aesthetic and Cultural Representation

Edited by

Murali Sivaramakrishnan

Published by

7/22, Ansari Road, Darya Ganj,
New Delhi-110002
Phones : +91-11-40775252, 23273880, 23275880, 23280451
Fax : +91-11-23285873
Web : www.atlanticbooks.com
E-mail : orders@atlanticbooks.com

Branch Office
5, Nallathambi Street, Wallajah Road,
Chennai-600002
Phones : +91-44-64611085, 32413319
E-mail : chennai@atlanticbooks.com

ISBN 978-81-269-1625-2

Printed in India at Glorious Printers, A-13, D.S.I.D.C., Jhilmil Industrial Area, Delhi-110095

Preface

The essays in this book were first presented at a national seminar on the Dynamics of Representation held in Trivandrum in January 2003 and jointly organized by the Centre for South Indian Studies, and the Indian Institute of Advanced Study, Shimla. I was then a Fellow at the Nehru Memorial Museum and Library, Teen Murti, New Delhi, and the venue of the proposed seminar was so far away. The pressures of time and space were serious constraints. However, so devout and dedicated were the handful of enterprising intellectuals who constituted the Centre for South Indian Studies, that virtually everything for the event—from the exotic venue at the Vyloppili Samskriti Bhavan to the various sessions and functions—was made possible through their combined effort and that too, within an amazingly short period. Prof. V.C. Srivastava, the then Director of the Indian Institute of Advanced Study, was the inspiring force behind the whole event. In a way, it may not be out of place to mention that there was virtually no difference between the organizers and the participants. It was, indeed a collective enterprise. My role was primarily to coordinate the various academic sessions and this task was indeed a smooth sailing one, mostly due to the unstinted support and intellectual benevolence of each of those who contributed to the seminar. The theme offered so much scope for rethinking culture, literature and arts. And the intellectual climate at the turn of the millennium had also tendered the right sort of theoretical contexts and the adequate terminology. It was a time to think about the acts of literary and aesthetic representations self-reflexively.

The book throws light on various aspects of literature, culture, post-modernism, colonialism, creativity and social transformation. It will be useful to the students and teachers of English literature as well as researchers of aesthetic and cultural representations in literature.

There are indeed many who I should thank. The Indian Institute of Advanced Study, Shimla made a generous gesture in terms of financial support that made it all possible. The Centre for South Indian Studies, Trivandrum made it all happen. The innumerable friends and well-wishers who did so much from behind the scene expecting nothing in return except perhaps their self-satisfaction of having done something for a cause, deserve so much credit. After all, it is certainly because of such generosities that we live on and are able to dream still. Without these, nothing!

Murali Sivaramakrishnan

Contents

Introduction

We live and move amidst sights and sounds. What we make of our lives depends a lot on the way we read meaning and significance in these. Moreover, there are other signs and symbols—both visual and verbal—that we deliberately create in order to communicate with ourselves as well as with others. These constitute our representations of the world around us. However, acts of representation need not always dissociate us from the world as it presents itself to us. The process could also lead us back towards a symbiotic relationship or engagement with our existence in the world.

What we normally understand by culture is a document composed of specific signs, sounds and symbols. And some of these are self-reflexive representations consciously and deliberately conceived. That ours is a world contaminated by the ingenuous association, combination and even banal confusion of multifarious signs, sounds and symbols is a tactile fact for which we need not seek farther than our own individual responses for corroboration. How do we make sense of this situation? Do we need to make any efforts at all, or is it a natural process? How do we go about reading and re-reading the represented image? Some of these queries would take us back to the ontological questions of art, literature and aesthetic representation. And this forms the general atmosphere of these essays.

Reading into representations, we can make some sense of our culture and metaphysics. The manner and mode of our reading or re-reading would also contribute to the significance of the acts of representations. Culture transforms and is transformed through such representations. History and ideology also contribute to representations. Representation is thus a combination of sign, sense and meaning. In their own ways, these essays engage with some of these issues in their various dimensions.

Contemporary theoretical discourse has introduced into our cultural practice, concepts such as centre, periphery, text, context, differance, alterity, subversion, transgression and the like. These have in turn triggered new intellectual vibrancy into the general slackening of dynamics and direction that followed in the wake of the modernist movement of the sixties and the political radicalism of the seventies, more so in south India. There also exists simultaneously a transverse concern for a new nationalism/internationalism with its consequent ambivalent attitude towards the post-colonial western-style modernizing of society, state and the nation. How does our cultural practices respond to these? What is their present status? Is there a need for the cultural idiom to be excessively concerned with theoretical issues? What is the role of critical theory and practice in the contexts of Indian literary and artistic representations? Is there already a strong intellectual movement to subvert and turn the centre-periphery model inside out? What has happened to the tentative attempts—those probings and explorations towards a common Indian poetic/aesthetic—towards the retracing of regional ideology and narrative? How do problems related to region, language and culture operate in the larger framework of nation, religion, spirituality and the narrative? Where and how do problems of region and environment, gender and ethnicity, figure in these? These are among the many questions that the essays contained in this book attempt to formulate answers for, in their various ways. By incorporating the works of creative writers and critical thinkers, the volume hopes to throw significant light on these issues. After all, no statement can achieve that finality of truth, and every act of representation is but an attempt in this direction.

The opening essay, "Breaking the Bowl of Clay: The Dynamics of Representation" argues that our present-day world is fabricated into being by the extremely sophisticated media that is an offshoot of technology. We are living in a virtual reality, not only on account of the complexities of our media culture, but also due to the inordinate flux of economic and market values into our ontological framework. In short, contemporary culture has come to be profoundly commercial. Mass produced market-oriented values dominate us and control and manipulate every aspect of our lives. The television and the Internet have come to represent primarily the commodity culture alongside the big-moneyed film industry. They churn out so-called popular images of culture fetishizing the same as the supremely valuable commodity. In the words of Walter Benjamin, "Culture has equally become profoundly economic or commodity oriented!" Perhaps, it is the developing countries more than the so-called developed ones that face the mighty presence of the cyber world. For, the process of production in a post-industrial situation has been for the developed countries, a process historically necessitated (through the feudal to the monarchical and post-renaissance enlightenment, industrial revolution, etc.) while the developing countries did not have to evolve through such similar paradigms in order to access a globally shared technological know-how. Nevertheless, in our present-day world, one cannot segregate even cultural crisis. We share our technologies and we share our crises very much like we share our air and our skies, or water. Nowadays, the television has come to represent our reality for us. Even the veracity of an incident gains its validity only when represented through this medium. Reality has become virtual. Semioticians and culture critics have time and again reminded us that any representation is more than what it represents, more than merely a reproduction of what it represents, and it also contributes to the construction of reality. The essay goes on to draw attention to the cultural implications of these issues. The contemporary aesthetic cannot be dissociated from history and the socio-cultural reality. There does exist a dialectical relationship between the represented and the real. Therefore, the inverted virtual image that our commercial culture parades through our present-day visual media only serves to distance us further from the real. The discussion is organized under four heads: the dynamics of representation; representation and cultural dialectics; representing the real; and representation and value contents, but in order to reorient ourselves towards our forfeited human values, we need to break our idols as much as our delusions. The begging bowl of clay needs to be shattered. The spiritual is the most dynamic and therefore the real.

Ashokamitran is an Indian writer in Tamil of renown and recognition. His "Literature, Culture and Society: A Writer's Responses", is indeed a personalized response to the cultural scenario of the Tamil country. He points out that writing in Tamil has not been able to keep the momentum and dynamic that was set forth by the Siddha writers, beginning with Sivavakkiar, which although largely spiritual and metaphysical, held the seeds for further replenishment. However, the literature of the last one hundred and fifty years could be seen to provide a record of a dialectical relationship with history and society of this part of the world. The essay is set forth in a personalized narrative tone and inquires further into this relationship between literature and contemporary culture.

Ayyappa Paniker, in his "Vive la Difference—Imperialism, Colonialism, Post-colonialism: Challenges to Cultural Plurality", speaks about culture and imperialism in the context of colonization. He uses the term 'imperialism' to refer to the attitudes and behaviour patterns of a culture that exercises hegemony of some kind or the other on cultures different from itself. The term colonialism, as he points out, could then be used to the situation of a culture that is dominated by another culture. One of these is identified in terms of assumed superiority which does not brook any questioning by the other, while the other is tacitly assumed to be the recipients of the so-called benefits of contact with the dominant culture. The two are conceived as opposites and the relationship is dialectical. The colonization of the country is followed by the colonization of the subject population, and this invariably colonializes the culture too. Hegemonial acceptance of the behavioural patterns of the superior culture undermines the indigenous one. Even now in the context of globalization, there looms large the threat of homogenization that wipes out all differences. Information technology seems to pave the path of standardization, until a counter-technology is developed which will control the tendency towards homogenization of cultures.

In "Premodern 'Superstitions'—A Counternormative Approach", M. Ramakrishnan, argues that the contours that demarcate the modern from the premodern are the conceptual creations of modernity motivated by a deep-rooted myth rather than the logic of objective analysis. In the latter-day view that postmodernism affords, the divide can be seen as actually emerging from the modernist tendencies to historicism propped on binary oppositions like man/nature, mind/matter, male/female, etc. The essay goes on to contextualise certain premodern "beliefs" that would be shelved as merely local or folk, and problematises them. It suggests that historically received knowledge from the traditional societies need to be seen in newer perspectives as sacred and valuable.

Madhusudhana Rao's "Places Without Roadmaps: Significance of 'Place' in the Postcolonial Discourse" focuses on the simultaneous existence of place and language as means of identity in post-colonial discourse. This takes place at two levels in recent Indian fiction in English: First, it becomes a presence in the writer's mind in creating the mood and guiding the narrative destiny; second, it becomes a means of internalizing the self and place for the personal satisfaction of the writer. The essay goes on to explore the imaginary homelands in Salman Rushdie's fiction.

Any effort to reconstruct or deconstruct women's discourse from the historical past would bring up questions regarding methodology and cultural constructs. Issues such as the authenticity of the women's voice and the socio-cultural framework of the utterance would of necessity surface. Usha V.T. in "Voices Behind the Veil: Representing Bhakti" draws attention to these theoretical issues while contextualising the discourse of the women mystics of medieval south India. She asks: "Does representing the personal as the public necessarily exclude the mainstream? Was the notion of invisibility foregrounded in order to subvert the voices behind the veil? Or was it the notion of valorizing silence as a desirable feminine trait that precluded women's utterances from being heard?" Usha explores the concept of woman's space within the religio-cultural sphere through a close reading and analysis of the writings of two women mystics, Andal and Akka Mahadevi.

Guillermo Rodriguez Martin, in his essay, "Modern Indian Poetry in English: Some Critical Issues", reflects on the situation of modernity in the context of Indian poetry in English. He examines critical positions like questions of identity, idea of nation and nationality, region and the narrative. He feels that in order to come to terms with ideas of modern and the post-modern, we need to re-frame our own literary contexts and cultural history.

In "The Story of My Experiements with Writing Life: Problematizing the Feminine Pen?", B. Chandrika, better known through her Malayalam pen-name Chandramathi, writes of her own attempts from quite early in life to be honest and truthful to experience. Reflecting on her writing career, she feels that the social contexts have perhaps become less frozen in our own times and this loosening of rigidity could account for the greater reach of contemporary writers, especially the woman writers. Fiction, she observes, could offer the best way to counter the forces of dominance and de-stability.

Lalitha Lenin considers the advent of postmodernism in the contexts of information and communication technology. "Theoretical Perspective of Subalternity: A Different Approach to Literature and Culture" is thus a re-examination of critical issues in this direction. In her view, the power that the advent of postmodernism signifies—the subaltern and the *dalit*—might prove to be quite fruitful in the future.

Postmodern concepts caught on in fashionable literary circles in Kerala quite early. However, they only added to the welter and confusion in intellectual and creative terms, argues M.G.S. Narayanan in his "Modernism, Post-modernism, Creativity and Colonialism in Malayalam Literature". The essay goes on to argue that the end of imitation marks the beginning of creativity. It is the dearth of creativity that marks the advent of hypocritical self-asseverations and fashionable jargons. For Narayanan, the recourse to almost all contemporary critical jargons in the historical context of contemporary Malayalam writing reveals but the insufficiency of the wellsprings of creativity.

Raman Nair's essay "British Intervention and Development of People's Information Systems in Kerala" is an overall view of the status and development of libraries in this part of the world and how intimately they are linked to the culture.

Usha Bande, in her article "Representing Culture, Repossessing History: Cultural Nuances in Three Indian English Novels", argues that the cultural implication of the colonial experience is one of the significant aspects of literary studies in the postcolonial period. She cites Fanon's observation that colonialism not only enslaves people politically, but also devalues their precolonial history, thus invading their culture and the present. The essay goes on to make a study of three works of fiction in order to examine how the authors reclaim their identity by remapping their cultural territory, and how, by reverting to the traditional narrative strategies they work out an indigenous framework.

"The Theatre of Protest in Kerala" signaled in more ways than one, the emerging political consciousness in the people. Vayala Vasudevan Pillai's essay provides an overall view of the development of the political theatre of the seventies and eighties in Kerala. As he shows, the theatre was directed at enlightening the common man and at questioning the so-called "upper class and the elite" on contemporary issues directly concerned with peace, food, freedom and social justice, irrespective of caste, creed and sex. The German master Bertolt Brecht and several other innovators have been instrumental in shaping this spirit of enquiry and self-reflexivity on aspects of the stage and performance.

Enrique Cámara de Landa's "Three Perspectives for the Study of Hybridization in the Italian Tango", is an interesting case study of the hybridization of the Argentinian Tango in the Italian culture. Fundamentally identifed with its place of origin, this dance form has undergone much transformation(s) and cross-cultural diffusions. The analysis of the structural traits in the

Italian tango reflects, as Enrique Camara shows in his study, the product of an interaction of the various elements—suppression, substitution, transformation, etc.

In the final analysis, I hope, these essays in their various ways reveal, the multifarious aspects of representation and its dynamics in culture, literature and the arts. And as I remarked at the beginning, their prime momentum lies in the pursuit of those ontological questions in terms of cultural and aesthetic representation.

I wish to acknowledge the help of all the contributors. Their patience and cooperation deserve special mention.

Murali Sivaramakrishnan

1

Breaking the Bowl of Clay: The Dynamics of Representation—Contexts of Cultural Situation(s) Dialectics, Social Transformation and Value

S. Murali

In a recent newspaper write-up, a historian and culture critic observed:

> Charged times require calm contemplation. The greater the din made by the forces of hate, the deeper the need for poetry, song, philosophy, for pursuing those questions that disturb the assumptions to which we cleave(?) The outpouring on the internet and in the media post-Gujarat, is the uprising of precisely such a desire to think, rethink, speak out again and again, in the name of our humanity, or to draw on spiritual vernacular, our Divine potential.... Death can and must provoke us to see clearly and live fully. Even in the deadliest hour, truth can reveal itself. (*The Hindu*, Sunday, December 15, 2002, p. 7)

Doubtless, the fact-guide that our newspapers and media have become, not only keep us constantly updated but also on our toes. There is no dearth to information in the present. Everyone is apparently equally well informed. Questions of what how and for whom and with regard to the mode, method, medium and the rationale of what is communicated notwithstanding, we can boast about our well-informed times. Every moment is to be seen with relation to an event of global relevance. We are used to the jargon of 'post'—post renaissance, post-September 11, now post-Gujarat. And what is not but post "post"? We tend to live in a continuous post-post but not in the present. And yet, despite all these well-informed humans, what we apparently have misplaced is our humanity! The media informs us about every happening which is consequential or inconsequential and we respond to everything with the same nonchalance with which we watch a popular serial; 'interspaced with loud jingles and commercials that also inform us about our compulsive need to buy this and not that, whether we need to or not. We are caught in the midst of channel wars—this is a helpless situation, a crisis of identity. Our choice is reduced to either Pepsi or Coca Cola and we have no other choice but to reach out for one simply because no one compels us to drink water. No one would deny that we are living through troubled times, we have apparently mastered the art of inflicting pain and suffering on a hitherto unprecedented scale on each other. No country is free from the deadly gator-grip of terrorism. An impending doom of genocide gathers like a cloud in our skies. Perhaps, we will only stop when we have succeeded in wiping out all life from the face of the earth-along with out own selves and the entire earth. And yet we go on living in a virtual reality, arranging and readjusting our life surfing across channels.

A very bleak future indeed! Crisis, human history has always confronted, but never in the present scale. Complexity has evolved to such magnitude that we no longer know what is what; each of us embody Orwell's vision of "double think" in grotesque individual variations.

Now, to recall what I cited at the beginning: these troubled times call for the soothing touch of the spirit. Charged times require calm contemplation. *The greater the din made by the forces of hate, the deeper the need for poetry, song, philosophy....* This is not to demean our technology or our visual media. It is a well-recognized fact that to sing one must have a song in one's heart—but now we have mislaid our songs. How can we resuscitate the life-giving springs within ourselves? Where do we begin? What are the positive signs of our times? How are they represented in the soothing mode of poetry and a philosophy of life?

To believe Fredric Jameson, economics has come to overlap with culture. Even without entering into the deadly fray of theories and counter-theories about the modern and the postmodern, one can safely accept this point. In an essay entitled 'End of Art' or 'End of History'?, he writes:

> ...everything including commodity production and high and speculative production and high and speculative finance, has become cultural; and culture has equally become profoundly economic or commodity oriented.
>
> (Jameson, Fredric. *The Cultural Turn*, London: Verso, 1998, p. 73)

I would like to add that not only has economics entered the cultural fabric but it has also come to dominate and function as a mainstay. It is indeed economics that now leads the way. Our values have come to be conditioned by market values. And only what is marketable finds place in the value systems. The TV and Internet have come to represent primarily the commodity culture alongside the big-moneyed film industry. Now here is some space for making some quick bucks as well. They churn out so-called popular images of culture fetishizing the same as the supremely valuable commodity. "Culture has equally become profoundly economic or commodity oriented!" perhaps it is the developing countries more than the so called developed that face the mighty presence of the cyber world. For, the process of production of a post industrial situation has been for the developed countries a process historically necessitated (through the feudal to the monarchical and post renaissance enlightenment, industrial revolution etc.), while the developing countries did not have to evolve through the similar paradigms in order to reach a globally shared post-technological knowhow. Nevertheless, in our present day world, one cannot segregate even cultural crises! We share our technologies and we share our crisis very much like we share our air and our skies. Jameson is not out of place in south India!

Bhopal, Chernobyl, Ayodhya, September 11th and Gujarat are all on the same side of local paper. There is no otherside.

One cannot even imagine a time not so far away when one did not have access to the internet and e-mail. Some years ago, my son, then barely six asked me to "speak to him about those good old times when you had to walk all the way across the room to flick the channel button!" He could never imagine a time when the remote was not there at all. The history of television and the rise of the channel wars in our part of the world are the history of re-representation of the visual and articulated image; they have reorganized our reality for us. Information and the process of dissemination of cultural representation all have undergone tremendous upheavals with this. The coming of the TV has ushered in a paradigm shift in our frames of reference. I would like draw attention to the drastic changes ushered in by the wave of television-created imagery. In the context of Kerala the eighties was a period of turbulent change followed by a steady stream of soap operas in the nineties. The Malayalee has learned to see himself and herself on the small screen and visualize regional history in the framework erected by the popular visual images. The TV supplies the past, present, and future. What is there on television today is significant: what is not there is naturally not so.

The point I wish to highlight is the easy adaptation of a popular cultural framework by the television medium. The Asianet at its inception attempted to reframe nostalgia for a misplaced political past of Kerala by recapturing the favourite songs from the people's theatre ventures of KPAC and old film songs. In fact the very film industry at its inception in the early fifties had attempted to adopt and adapt Malayalam fiction very much in this faction: the works of major Malayalam writers were recast in to the film mould. What was important then was just to retell the tale in a different medium. It took quite some time for the film industry to realize its own potential for representing. Film language was there for the discovery—an entire field in itself! A new aesthetic was in the offing. The medium grew out of all proportions and instead of being tamed it has come to tame people at large. It is a case of the subject subjecting the student into subjugation. The television has developed out of all proportions like the little Brahmin in the fabled tale of Mahabali.

Nowadays the television has come to represent the reality for us. Even when we need to verify the validity of some incident or happening we ask: was it shown on TV? As if represented on the TV reality becomes more real for us!

The theoreticians of semiotics as well as theoretically sophisticated sociologists and culture critics have time and again reminded us that *any representation is more than what it represents, more than merely a reproduction of what it represents: it also contributes to the construction of reality!*

Now we have come to inhabit a world fabricated into being by the technological media. We are living in a virtual reality. Not only on account of the complexities of the medium but also due to the inordinate influx of economic and market values into our ontological framework.

In the *Mahabharata*, a Yaksha asks Yudhistira to name the most mysterious thing in the world and Yudhistira replies: The most mysterious thing is man. All around us we find everything falling, failing, dying and yet the amazing thing is that we go on living, disregarding the fact of death and decay!

In all probability, human kind cannot bear very much reality. We need to hide our heads under the sand like the ostrich when it comes to dangerous *situations*. We are great self-deceivers. Our safety lies in our delusions. Hence the convenience of the TV and its fabricated delusive world. Soap operas do not make so much demands on our brain. Let us be passive and let life pass by....

This is not to mean that technology by itself is to be blamed for our present crisis. Neither is it intended to heap complaints on the techno-media. It is the culpability of those who allow themselves to be entangled by the surface superficial textures of both that I challenge as leading to this techno-mess. True, popular culture is democratic and pluralistic; it does away with all distinctions of high and low art and addresses the common woman. But then, too much of that mere entertainment industry unconcerned *with those old fashioned questions* of values has brought us to this artful mess; we only believe in the virtual. Perhaps this is the result of the "coca-colonization" of culture.

How do we go on inhabiting a world well nigh virtual, where the borderlands of dream, fantasy and commerce merge inextricably into one long unending chain. The Yaksha is standing bewildered and both Yudhistira and Mahakavi Vyasa are staring at each other. This is not magical realism. This is reality for us. It is sometimes an Ayodhya, a September 11 or a Gujarat that give us a shake. Shall we dig within for a clear stream of spirituality, for sanity, for humanness?

"Make it new," was the slogan of European Modernists. Fredric Jameson writes:

> Let us spend our time on the bad new things, Brecht joyously recommended, and
>
> Let the good old things bury themselves; yet the passion and the praxis of actuality evidently proves less usable when the very sense of what constitutes actuality becomes confused and aimless... The Brechtian new would then, today, turn out to be just another of those "good old things" he suggested we do away with. (pp. 93-94)

To believe in this view of Jameson is not to be too prudish and take sides against the contemporary shifting sense of values at the same time insisting on rigidity in our value systems. The creative psyche will always necessarily be on the move in a state of constant dynamis never getting stranded in any period. However, in our times in this part of the world, the virtual reality is shrouded by market values and passes for I the real. Probably, this is where we need to get our bearings relocated and our value systems readjusted. The Yaksha of the Mahabharata is again posing conundrums. The Postmodern as well as the modern for us are not historical product of late capitalism they are not historically necessitated but transplanted from overseas as mental ideas. Hence defamiliarising ourselves is the only possibility of release from this gator grip of those recurrent waves of colonization. We have to realize that the dream world created by the mass hysterical visual media is not real—neither does it represent the desired reality for us. It is a substitute world wherein we are the opium eaters. Is religion the only opium of the masses in the present?

We need to break our idols like way back in the sixties. Charged times require calm contemplation. The greater the din made by the forces of hate, the deeper the need for poetry, song, philosophy.... When fundamentalism reigns supreme and the forces of fascism are unleashed, it is the need of the hour to think about breaking the idols. When we start killing each other in the name of religion, it is time to rethink religious values and sing and dance after the idol is broken. It will not merely do to sit back and watch those startling images of massacre and inhuman cruelty—what man in doing to man—these times plead for us to be come more self aware—jagrata, jagrata. In more ways than one spirituality is irreligious; the spiritual is boundless and unconditional, it is dynamic and vibrant and holds nothing sacred including the sacred.

There is an old Tamil song that was quite popular at one time. It goes like this:

Nanda vanathil oru andi
Avan arezhu nalaka koyavanai vendi
Kondu vandan oru thondi

Athai kondadi kondadi
Pott utai thandi
Nanda vanathil oru andi

(*The Begging Bowl of Clay*)

An andi there was
In Nandavanam
Who prayed and prayed
At the potter's door
For days on end to get
A begging bowl of clay
He danced with joy
All the way back

With his begging bowl of clay
He danced with it
In sheer delight
That he dropped
His begging bowl of clay.
He broke
The begging bowl of clay.

(**Andi:** a mendicant beggar often a bhakta of the Lord Shiva. In another version, "kondadi" is replaced by "Koothadi" that clearly refers to Lord Shiva who is held to be "the dancer").

This I believe is representation at the peak of its dynamis. The breaking of the bowl is breaking the magic circle of the virtual and a reaching after the true, the vast the beautiful.

Every age had had its voice of conscience in the poet. In almost any age and in every climate we come across writing that rues the day.... "the time is out of joint, O cursed sprite..." (Shakespeare, *Hamlet*) "Who, if I cry, would hear me among the angelic orders? (Rilke, *Duino Elegies*)

Some years ago, in connection with the birth centenary celebrations of the great Malayalam poet Vallathol Narayana Menon, there was a national Seminar on Indian Renaissance. It was a gathering of many well-known intellectuals. There was a widespread apprehension and genuine concern over the then too apparent cultural and spiritual stagnation. In their preliminary note the seminar organizers wrote:

> This spiritual and cultural stagnation seems to have become so deeply entrenched that when the emergency was clamped down upon the nation, there was no whimper of protest from those sections of the intellectuals from whom one could have naturally expected sharp reactions. Perhaps it should be said that the emergency itself represented the lowest depths of the spiritual degradation and moral stagnation. It seems the time has come for an indepth reappraisal of these questions, especially in view of the clouds of a fascist menace looming large over the Indian national horizon.

(Govindan, M. "The Menace of Fascism and the Indian Intellectual", *Indian Renaissance*, ed. K. Ayyappa Paniker, Trivandrum, 1993, p. 34.)

Very foreboding thoughts these. In his invited response, M. Govindan, the noted Malayam intellectual, astutely pointed out that the crisis in the cultural and social sphere is largely on account of our negligence to perceive the integrated nature of the material and the spiritual. Discussing the terrors and the menace of fascism and the Indian intellectual he said: I think, renaissance is a kind of balance between the body and the soul—otherwise there cannot be a rebirth. I believe this is as true of the present as then—this delicate and fine balance. Somewhere in our blind march in the desacralised times towards a postmodern, a post-technological post, post India, we appear to have left our hearts behind. Again, it is a request for the misplaced balance, a quest for values. Their virtual reality has blinded us, we need to break free. Break the bowl.

Representation and Cultural Dialectics

We have come to inhabit a world fabricated into being by the technological media. We are living in virtual reality. Not only on account of the complexities of the medium but also due to the inordinate influx of economic and market values into our ontological framework. The mass produced metaphors of this commercial culture tells us how to live in accordance with these market values. We accommodate ourselves to this commodity fetish, to this surreality. Here the aesthetic is not in any way removed from the historical and the socio-cultural. What is represented on our small screens reorganizes our reality for us. This is a dream world, but not the dream world engendered by poetry and art. The cyber-romance is not the creative romantic of the poet and artist. I would like to draw a distinction between these. Poetry and art essentially lead us towards a better humanity, towards a better world in spite of the deconstructionist's warning with regard to the politico-social density of the language of images and words. There is a world out there that is humane wherein we can suffer the voice of our neighbour and even enjoy it like music! There we do recall those dislocated values of sorority, fraternity, love and tolerance. These are not only for the saints. They are for all. As Octavio Paz, in a wild fury of metaphorical language describes poetry:

> Poetry is knowledge, salvation, power, abandonment. An operation capable of changing the world, poetic activity is revolutionary by nature; a spiritual exercise, it is a means of interior liberation. Poetry reveals this world; it creates another. Bread of the chosen; accursed food. It isolates, it unites. Invitation to the journey, return to the homeland. Inspiration, respiration, muscular exercise Prayer, litany, epiphany, presence. Exorcism, conjuration, magic. Sublimation, compensation, condensation of the unconscious. Historic expression of races, nations, classes. It denies history... Madness, ecstasy, logos. Return to childhood, coitus, nostalgia for paradise, for hell, for limbo. Play, work, ascetic activity. Cofession, Innate experience, Vision, music, symbol. (*The Bow and the Lyre*, Austin and London: Univ. of Texas, 1973. p. 3)

It has been the contention of many artists and poets around the world that the entire history of poetry could be seen as an index of the expanding human awareness.

This is not to mean that there has been a logical and linear expansion—poetry does nothing like that. There is a deep felt link between the poet and the people. To believe Czeslaw Milosz, poetry has always followed "the mysterious movements of the great soul of the people".

> That sacred art of the word, just because it springs forth from the sacred depths of Universal Being, appears to us bound, more rigorously than any other mode of expression, to the spiritual and physical movement of which it is a generator and a guide... Sacerdotal in prehistoric times epic at the moment of Greek colonial expansion, psychological and tragic at the decline of the dionysia, Christian, theological and sentimental in the Middle ages, neoclassical since the beginning of the first spiritual and political revolution—namely the renaissance—finally romantic...poetry has

> always followed, fully of its terrible responsibilities, the mysterious movements of the great soul of the people...
>
> (*The Witness of Poetry,* Massachusetts: Harvard Univ Press, 1983)

The last three decades of the last century saw amazing changes in the literary and artistic sensibility of south India in particular. Much like during the period of the Bhakti revival (which has of late come into serious critical debates in the context of evaluating cultural values and artistic revival or renaissance) it was mostly in the south Indian languages that the earliest seeds of modernism burst forth. Tamil, Kannada, Marathi, Telugu and Malayalam poetry chartered out regions of the new. Ezra Pound's call to "Make it New" resounded here in this part of the world albeit slightly! later than in Europe and America. Modernism came in the form of breaking of the shackles. The literary and artistic form underwent drastic changes. However, the modern was not something that was historically necessitated as in the west but an aesthetic idea/ideal that was transplanted hurriedly from alien soil. Nevertheless it survived. For instance, the trajectory of modernist poetry in Malayalam can be seen as striking a parallel to the rampant spread of market capitalism and commodity culture, although capitalism in Kerala did not evolve naturally from the social context; capitalist and feudalist values survived side by side not excluding each other. The physical living conditions of the people became altered and a new concept in space surfaced as cities became overcrowded and more urbanized. Perhaps the insight of the Marxist critic Christopher Caudwell would serve better to explicate this situation although the observation was directed in a different context. In his *Illusion and Reality*, 1937, Caudwell wrote:

> Poetry reaches technically an unprecedented competence; it draws more and more apart from reality... the great mass of men no longer read poetry, no longer feel the need for it, no longer understand it, because poetry has moved away from concrete living by the development of its technique and this movement was itself only the

counterpart of a similar movement in the whole of society.

The poet came to be more and more isolated from his people on account of the hieratic nature of his utterance. However, there was a general make-belief that the times demanded change in form and content. The late seventies and early eighties witnessed a tremendous spurt of creativity in Malayalam and Tamil writings as well. *Puthu Kavithai and adhunikatha* were of like concern for the Tamil and Malayalee. The need of the times was to relocate the self. This was also the period of translation: many voices from around the globe reechoed in this part of the world garbed in the local language. Pablo Neruda and Frantz Kafka, Bertolt Brecht and Paul Clean, Herman Hesse and Yvgene Yevtushenko, Octavio Paz and Ranier Maria Rilke, the list is endless. This was the case in fiction and drama alike. New writing came to be. A new dynamics of form set in. This period also witnessed a rise in political radicalism side by side. Gone were the romantic revolutionaries of the fifties and sixties; here were poets who were self-reflexive articulators of new found ideological voice. Malayalam poetry perked up and the new diction was easily imbibed by a sahrdaya, Kavi Arangu were the order of the day. Poets like Kadammanitta Ramakrishnan, Balachandran Chullikkadu, Punalur Balan, D Vinayachandran, Ayyuappa Paniker, ONV Kurup, Sugatha Kumari and others could draw huge crowds of young and enthusiastic admirers who carried on reciting their works even after they stopped reciting. More than ever the poetic voice, the Dravidic rhythms and the charisma of the poets achieved newer dimensions. This could very well be looked upon as the most dynamic period in the history of Malayalam poetry. Here the poet became the voice of the people's conscience. She was the kavi, the drsta in the proper sense of the term. The rise of print capitalism and the rise of the new wave of modernism in Malayalam writing almost appear to go hand in glove. If in the seventies it was the delight of discovering new forms of narratives, in the eighties it was the refraction of the image, a kind of ironical radicalism, a self-reflexive voice, a new sound of social sense. However, this intimacy between the creator and the reader/listener, between the poet and his sahrdaya was not to remain long. The late eighties ushered in the newer post modernwave. Strange as it might appear, among the languages of the south, the most adamant and thus posing the most resistance to change are Tamil and Malayalam and yet, these are the two languages that easily succumbed to the onslaught of what Wole Soyinka in another context has described as the *second wave of colonization*: that is Theory. As early as the late seventies literary theory hit our academic circles; but it took quite some time to seep into the creative psyche of the south Indian writer. Cultural activities had always found the intellectual atmosphere of the universities and other academic circles congenial for their growth. So was the case with modernist Malayalam poetry; it had an academic childhood and manhood. Confronted with the new fangled ideas of the semioticians and structuralists with regard to the challengeable role of language in its efficacy of articulating the truth of the world and the veracity of the literary and aesthetic image as being a derivative sign, the creative writer became more inward looking in her act of dealing out words and images. Did the word come first or did it but replace the prior image? Where does experience figure beside these? Is experience itself a product of our linguistic universe? However, such an interface never actually surfaced in Malayalam. What really would serve to demarcate a shift in modernist sensibilities in the nineties is the nascent awareness of the voice of the subaltern—the dalit and the woman, hitherto unheard and unseen surfaced with renewed energy. Of course, this is not to deny their presence until then—the downtrodden and the woman had been historically marginalized and had to be consciously brought back into the societal consciouness.

Although there was a deep felt worry whether one should articulate one's creative experience through the newly found sensibility of altercation and artifice, literary theory did not leave a scarred surface on the face of the regional writing from south India. On the other hand, literary criticism was drastically affected by theory from the west. Many concepts and notions were bodily lifted and transplanted in the regional mental geography without any critical examination of their cultural context or roots. Theory came to be applied left and right indiscriminately as a tool for analysis. Writers have come to feel a certain sense of inadequacy if they are not able to air a few neocritical terms flamboyantly to reveal their schooling and class. Applicability and relevance were never considered; fashion was to be erudite and knowledgeable. The malleability and ductility of theoretical speculation probably would account for this easy transplant. Print capitalism thrived further in this critical boom. The late eighties and nineties in Kerala for the most saw a boom in the previously dormant publishing industry. However, the effects of these activities were insignificant in comparison with the geometric progress of the television media. Very much like the regional channels, regional writing in the south has been through a severe struggle to come to terms with its own regional identity. Because when one is constantly playing with representations, one is bound to be confronted with such questions as: What are we representing? For whom are we representing? What is it that is represented and how does it represent what it is supposed to? These are not easy questions to be answered. But the fact that they have appeared at all is promising. If such a self-reflexivity were to manifest in our visual media, it would certainly augur a new horizon of hope.

The postmodern debate is quite rampant in the intellectual circles in this part of the world today. Questions of the nature of cultural identity, the interface between the modern and the postmodern are all debated. Whether one believes in Jurgen Habefrnas's theory that *postmodernity* is but an incomplete project of modernity, at all, one can perceive certain theoretical continuities in the attitudes to representations in our times, questions which have also been discussed by the high modernists. As a single instance, G. Aravindan's much popular cartoon strip of the sixties; Cheriya *Manushyarum Valiya Lokavum* that could on its own right represent the changing times during the onset of modernism presages many issues of the postmodern. But however, in our midst, we now have many who insist on being either modern or postmodern in outlook and life and living writing thinking and being without as much as turning a questioning glance at the relevance of such theorizing in our cultural context. They would fall easy prey to the lures of the tinsel world of the small screen—for its glamour and limelight are quite easily accessible too. A current trend on all channels is the big money winning quiz programme after the *Big's B's Kon Banega Crorepati* became a commercial hit. I will only pause to draw attention to the sort of simple questions that the participants are called upon to answer. The point is to make it easily accessible to the common man. Anyone can participate and everyone can make some quick bucks. Very democratic! Very postmodern too.

I have chosen three poems in Malayalam from three markedly different periods as signifying the changes in representation: one from the premodern times (the late forties and the trend continued up to the fifties as well), Vailoppilly Sreedhara Menon's *For Want of Rice*, one from the modern period = A Ayyappan's *Supper*, and the third, as signifying the woman's voice of the present = Vijayalakshmi's *Bhagavatham*. Here are the English versions of the three poems:

1

Ariyillanjitte For Want of Rice,
Vailoppillil Sreedhara Menon *Kannikoyttu*, 1947.

Those who cared not
When the poor soul lived
Came most willing
To shoulder his corpse.

Much indeed like the great
The lot of the commons on earth
For they too come to be most loved
After their death.

Some chop down the mango tree
Some clear the fence
And some by the bereaved widow sit
Comforting her.

Money by the compassion
Of a neighborhood manor came

That fetched a length of cloth
For the dead man's shroud.

Setting his betel box aside
An elderly gentleman marched in
To where the woman she lay
And busily announced.

Everything is OK
We have laid him down
And all we now need is some dried rice
To strew round the body.

Replied the bereaved widow
Her voice bitter and broken
If but we had rice
He wouldn't have died.

2

Supper, A. Ayyappan,

While the crowd stood
Treading the blood,
Of the wayfarer who died
In the accident.
My eyes rested on the five rupee note
That fluttered out of the dead man's pocket.
My wife—a grass widow, despite me.
My kids—scarecrows of hunger.

Let today's supper be with this.
Tonight—
Kids sleeping peacefully
With the taste of supper still in their mouths
With half empty-stomachs, me and my woman.

The dead man's post-mortem
Or cremation
Might be over....

With drooping heavy eyelids
Trying to recollect: the blood-treading crowd.

Dead
Dispensing
Consecrated bread
For the hungry living.

3

Bhagavatham, **Vijayalakshmi,** trans. **Satchidanandan.**

At dusk you take you holy dip
And away from the noises of the world,
You read aloud the sacred book,
Bhagavatha.

Why don't you come, come on
Listen—you keep calling me.
But I am busy by the fire,
Cooking the meal for you.
A hundred plates and pots
Remain to be washed
And a hundred little things,
Chores for tomorrow.

With, my soot-blackened hands
I turn the leaves of a mighty
Bhagavatha that will end
Only when my life ends
And willingly go on reading it,
But you never come to hear me.

For Want of Rice represents a still-unified community in the process of transformation, the decrepitude and the trauma of poverty and suffering. One individual's plight is represented through the evocative presentation of a tragic I situation. There is a certain directness of utterance and the language does not slip away into any disordering of the aesthetic sensibility. In Ayyappan's poem, the hungry man eyeing the fluttering five rupee note signifies the isolated image of the modern man. There is no organic community, there is only the individual and his personal greed. The image is stark and direct too. However, in the case of *Bhagavatham*, there is this implication of the woman's role in society; does she exist in the scheme of things at all? Does she ever play a significant role in society? In the process of the construction of reality, she is marginalized- she has been and she still is. The narrator is a woman, no doubt. Her male counterpart is self-assuredly livinga societally sanctioned life, reading the lord's life very devoutly and even inviting her to join him, completely unaware of her "real" life. It could even be read differently:

"Why don't you come and sit beside me and watch the Ramayana and Mahabharata on TV? It is so very religiously produced, you know!"

Representing the Real: The Transformnation of the Image

No image is created in isolation. No representation takes shape in a vacuum. Every represented image is an attempt to capture a moment in its fleeting existence. Writing for us, as much as painting to a certain extent is a dialogue between ourselves and the world out there. In more ways than one, it is a dialectical relationship: responding, interpreting, changing.

"Nature is on the inside" says Paul Cezanne. And the created image, whether it is eidetic, iconic or symbolic, is undeniably linked to the world out there and the world of sensations—or their echoes in our own body. Region, geography, representation and culture form one single continuous paradigm.

According to Arnold Hauser the radical sociologist,

> a work of art is a challenge, we draw upon our own aims and endeavours. In interpreting it, we draw upon our own aims and endeavours, inform it with a meaning that has its origin in our own ways of 'Life and thought'. In a word, any art that really affects us becomes to that extent modern art.
>
> (Hauser, "A Sociology of Art", *Re-Visions: New Perspectives on Art Criticism*. Ed. Howard Smagula. New Jersey: Princeton Hall, 1990, p. 15)

Seen in this light art is an order of signification common to mankind as a whole, and by virtue of its essential nature non-evolutive and non-progressive. In interpreting it from within ourselves, we enter into a dialectical relationship with the represented image. Historical distance, cultural and ethnic unfamiliarity drops away under a shared human awareness. The modern does not ask for specific form or specific content. When Rilke writes: who, if I cry would hear me among the angelic orders ("Duino Elegies"), or when Herman Hesse writes: And the entire history of my love/is you and this evening (Elizabeth), we who read them experience a totally meaningful universe of image, a gestalt or a multiverse, wherein we move in silence as through the caves of Ajanta or Ellora, with our mind's eye like a torch lighting up its walls. It does matter little whether we apprehend an ideal world of images or experience the concrete presence of the real mediated through allusion, allegory or symbol. What matters is that art creates for us a self-conscious other and invites us into that fictional world, a world of myth, of poetry, of icons and symbols, where we attain another self-consciousness through quite another reality. This is far from the dissolution of the thinking being in front of the TV, a mere passive receiver holding an inert remote sensor.

Primitive art was the representation of a mythological universe. Myth and form interface and the art of the primitive is the expression of the mythic conception of the world. For the cave man depicting the bison before the hunt, the image drawn is representative of the hunt and serves a magical function. Thus, one could say that in primitive societies poetry, incantation and painting served ritualistic functions. In a way, the work of art retained its sacredness and the image was held to be holy even after the basic ritual was over. The picture or icon of a deity serves a similar function. It is an object of aesthetic experience but it is charged with ritualistic and mystical significance—a post-ritualistic significance! In Dravidian culture, pictorial representations done in the three ritual modes—*Bhuta Vadivu*, *Chitra Vadivu* and *Silpa Vadivu*—are considered sacred and holy. Now, the breaking of a mirror wherein we see ourselves represented is looked upon as undesirable. The power of the created image is still largely in operation. The entire functioning of society and history depends on the transference of the created image. In our times, Banks and stock exchanges have taken over the act of representing images on currency notes, coins and the share markets. The most valuable are our societal images and roles. Our current deities are processed on the celluloid screens. We haven't marched much farther than our primitive ancestors; only our images have been transformed. The French artist Marcel Duchamp in 1917 sent in a urinal to an exhibition titled "Fountain". Through the inversion of this object and thereby draining its very functional meaning, he was obviously proposing a change of art/artist, object/public relationship. The *audi* of the popular Tamil song that I cited earlier also does a similar act. By gloating so much on the object of his affection, he goes to the extent of breaking its very form. It is a tragic situation as well. But the breaking of the mud bowl is the transference of the represented image, into its essential self. In Hindu death ceremony a mud bowl is intentionally broken in order to symbolize the unity of atman and Brahman. The broken mud bowl signifies the breaking of all forms and represents the unrepresentable. The need of our times is this breaking of the bowl of clay.

Representation and Value

Any act of representation involves an act of cultural embodiment, as we have already seen. Any representation is more than what it represents, and it also contributes to the construction of reality. There does exist a dialectical relationship between the representation and the real. Therefore, the inverted virtual image that our commercial culture parades through present day visual media only serves to distance us further from the reality. Ernst Gombrich has a theory of all art as illusion. However, as he would also agree the illusory image represents the real as much as twins resemble each other but cannot be said to represent each other. Similarly, reprints of a work of art in this age of technological reproduction resemble the work more than they present what they in the first place were to represent. So, in the endless repetition of visual images and signs that our times have given rise to, we have distanced ourselves from our essential reality (if at all there is something like that) and what is more, we reconstruct our world endlessly on those lines too. Once we recognize the technologically constructed images for what they are, they would become so transparent that we could see through them.

According to the Sanskrit aestheticians, the entire cosmos is an aesthetic representation: only as an aesthetic continuum could the cosmos be resolved. It is the dance of Siva. The experience of the aesthetic was considered to be a vivarta of the brahmic consciouness. Therefore, in the creative art of representation the artist/poet is the god-player. And far from leading the mind towards attachment to and possession of the world of things, people, experience and sensations, the aesthetic dissociates itself from the worldly and the corporeal. It is not an escape from reality but a holistic experience of the real. The shattering of the mud pot is the shattering of all shackles and the experience of the spiritual.

In the Isa Upanishad we read:

Isa vasyam idam sarvam
Yat kim ca jagatyam jagat
Tena tyaktena bhunjita
Ma grdhah kayasvid dhanam.

All this, whatever moves in this world is enveloped by God. Therefore, find your enjoyment in renunciation; do not covet what belongs to others. The Upanishad enjoins us to enjoy through abandonment, through distancing ourselves from the object of our enjoyment. Not in possession, but in aesthetic distancing is the relish, the ananda, the bliss of communion. *To have the mud pot, to hold it and dance, only later to drop it and shatter it.*

I would like to conclude with a small poem that would work as a Zen Koan. These are among the marvelous lines of poetry that my generation grew up with representing and re-representing our fears, anxieties, memories. This one is from Garcia L'orca, the Spanish poet. *I do not recall who did this translation*:

If I die
Leave open the window.

The boy eats oranges
(I'll see him from my window).

The reaper reaps the wheat
I (I'll hear him from my window).

If I die
Leave open the window.

References

Aravindan, G. *Cheriya Manushyarum Valiya Lokavum.* Strip Cartoons, Kottayam, D.C. Books, 1996.

Caudwell, Christopher. *Illusion and Reality* (1937). 1945.; Rpt. New Delhi: People's Publishing House, 1978.

Hauser, A. "Sociology of Art", *Re-Visions: New Perspectives on Art Criticism.* Ed. Smagula, Howard. New Jersey: Princeton Hall, 1990.

Jameson, Fredric *The Cultural Turn*, London: Verso, 1998.

Milosz, Czeslaw. *The Witness of Poetry.* Massachusetts: Harvard Univ. Press, 1983.

Paniker, K. Ayyappa (ed.). *Indian Renaissance*, New Delhi: Sterling, 1993.

Paz, Octavio. *The Bow and the Lyre.* Austin: Univ. of Texas, 1973.

Ramakrishnan, E.V. (ed.). *The Tree of Tongues*, Shimla: IIAS, 1998.

Usha VT "Gender Television and Society: A Case Study". *Studies in Humanities and Social Sciences*, Vol IX. No. 1. Summer 2002, pp. 33-58.

2

Literature, Culture and Society: A Writer's Response

Ashokamitran

As a writer of some fifty years standing and having had to face and interact with different kinds of readers (who are the truly the real justification for a writer), I must say that I am saddened when I reflect upon the relationship of literature and the possible slackening or heightening of forces of change or dynamism of Indian society. Maybe I can't call myself a valid representative of all writers of this country. My language which is Tamil is spoken by over sixty million people and can claim an antiquity of at least two thousand years of literature. In a sense, the language has maintained its contemporaneity with a minimum of modifications over these centuries. It is difficult to say that the literature in Tamil has been a faithful recorder of change but one can see it rather obliquely done, in certain works. The Siddha literature beginning with Sivavakkiar and for a few years afterwards does tell the forces of dynamism or change. But probably, that spirit could not prevail continuously and consistently because the major parts of Tamilnadu came under rulers of non-Tamil origins and it is very likely, that factor delayed a further flowering or development of the Siddha literature. Though its one aspect is strongly spiritual, the social aspect is rejecting the Brahmin outlook or attitude.

So, until about the 19th century with the literature being mainly ethical and didactic and again mostly in verse, reflection of social change at different periods could only be inferred. It is with the beginning of secular writing, especially creative writers in the middle of 19th century, that the dynamics of society came to be inevitably ingrained in the creative works. So, in these one hundred and fifty years, the writers could be faulted for incomplete pictures, lines towards one or other community or sect, but the creative writers in Tamil has nurtured itself upon the dynamics of social change.

But having asserted that the writers had not failed the society, what has been the role of the society? Here again, I limit myself to the language I belong to, i.e, Tamil. What in an assembly like this would be considered a worthwhile book of fiction or a collection of poems doesn't reach beyond a few thousand Tamil readers. Some fifty, sixty years ago when the modernist phase of writing was pursued rigorously by the Manikkodi group of writers—to name some of them, Ku Pa Rajagopalan, Padumaipition, Na Pichamurthy, C.S. Challappa—it was realized their writings enjoyed a readership of about ten thousand readers. Ka Naa Subramanian, who was most active as a writer or critic from 1936 to 1990 in one sixty years—for all this forceful advocacy of the better class of writers and denouncement of what was escapist or non-literary, felt that response from Tamil society for better creative writing always hovered around a few thousand readers.

Now more books are being written or published and it must follow that they are sold, and the purchasers read them but the writer is always in the back rows of society. I once again remind you that I am referring to the Tamil society. But in other aspects, the Tamil society has been most progressive is only when it responds to creative writing that one feels a little depressed.

There has been an explosion of Indian writing in English and some truly wonderful work is being done by the writers in the last twenty years. And they are from very different language groups though they write in English. Recently, I happened to read a few books written by Indians in English—these writers are all quite young—may be thirty or forty years younger than I—and their books are very good. *The Better Man* by Anita Nair, *Difficult Daughters* by Ranjan Kapur, the latest book of Amit Choudhuri (which won the Sahitya Akademi prize) are some of them. And of all Arundhati Roy. But for each of these works, I can think of an equally good or better work done in our language. We would say if we had a common critical aesthetic, all these books will become as celebrated as the ones written in English. But in reality, it does not happen that way. One who displays a heightened sense of critical faculty in the case of books in English, doesn't evidence the same calibre when it comes for a work done in Tamil. A standard solution offered is, get your books translated into English.

There really is a boom as regards translation from Tamil to English is concerned. And a few publishers are sympathetic for these translations, from 2000 to 2002. I would say more than a hundred books from the Indian languages have been translated into English.

These days most newspapers or magazines publish a list of best sellers, the data being collected from reputed bookshops. Whether it is Bombay or Hyderabad or Chennai, I am yet to find a translation in the best-seller list. The books written in English, yes. But not those translated into English from the Indian languages.

But probably, literature is not and cannot be a trustworthy index of a culture or society. Literature is one of the manifestations but not necessarily an all-embracing one. Even those wonderful books written by Indians in English show a world that looks like Indian society but one also has a lingering feeling that it is not adequate. R.K. Narayan wrote nothing else but about the small world he lived in. There are flashes of truth but not totally ratifying.

For a writer, I have talked too much. For all my efforts all my life for...what is called the self, it is that self that gets through to retain my work. And I find that the discipline of creative writing—if it be called a discipline, seems totally unsuitable for me for comment upon the important topics that are taken up for deliberation in this assembly. The scholars and researchers are better placed in this respect. People won't agree but that is the truth.

3

Vive la Différence! Imperialism, Colonialism, Post-colonialism: Challenges to Cultural Plurality

Ayyappa Paniker

I use the term 'imperialism' here to refer to the attitudes and behaviour patterns of a culture that exercises hegemony of some kind or other on cultures different from itself. The term colonialism could then be used to the situation of a culture that is dominated by another culture. One of these is identified in terms of assumed superiority which does not brook any questioning by the other, while the other is tacitly assumed to be the recipients of the so-called benefits of contact with the dominant culture. The two are conceived as opposites and the relationship is dialectical. The privileged culture, it is believed, bestows respectability on the under-privileged one. It has obviously greater military power, economic viability, and political authority, and hence establishes an influence on the other. Post-colonialism in this context will be understood as the condition of continuing, dependence or-servility, even when the imperial power may have physically withdrawal from the scene for the time being.

The imperial abuse of power is matched in degree by the colonial practice of Servility: in matters of culture, it involves the substitution, partial or wholesale, of alien forms of cultural expression and manifestation by the colonized. The colonization of the country is followed by the colonializers of the subject population, and this invariably colonializes the culture also. In the later 19th century and early 20th century, Indians in government offices and schools wearing a dhoti tucked around the waste, a shirt and tie, a coat, and often a turban or hat on the head, were a common sight in many parts of India. This motley could be seen as a regular feature not only in this bizarre costume, but also in the intellectual attitudes as well as the behavioural patterns among educated Indians. Educated in those days meant only trained in the western way in new model schools. The impact of imperialism on culture was thus institutionalized and was the most visible aspect of the hegemony of the British. The worship of everything British was built into the psyche of the educated Indians, who were happy to be willing slaves under the foreign masters. Some Babus continued to admire the British, like Nirad Choudhuri, who thought that there were no villages in India; for him, only the villages in England were real villages. Food habits too changed among the urban classes, and even food items assumed foreign names, which were considered civilized, sophisticated and tasty. Even foreign games, too, like cricket, acquired a respectability seldom conceded to native ones using stick and ball. Even gestures like nodding the head or shrugging the shoulders or waving the hand had to be borrowed along with the use of British idioms and received pronunciation, discarding the unwanted intrusions of substandard Indianisms. While the spokesmen of imperialism did whatever they liked without strict adherence to scruples ill the manner of Robert Clive, who probably laid the first stone of the British Empire in India, sometimes called Indian empire too. The legacy of the Commonwealth bestowed on the colonials and sometimes gleefully accepted by them as an honour, was bound to lose its tinsel glamour, when the "mother country" does not have the wherewithal to keep it going and maintain its relevance. All culture is hybrid by definition, but what is deplorable is the high and low status between the unequal partners on the parallel of the haves and have-nots, the pure and the impure, the mainstream and the marginal. This discrimination led to imbalance in cultural give and take, and what should ideally have been a close collaboration degraded into a donor and recipient relationship and vitiated the whole enterprise. The indiscriminate discrimination in the political power game affected the cultural scenario also and led to the depletion of national and native cultures. This is the kind of threat that underlies any attempt at oneway globalization, any one way of life being glorified as superior and standard, while all the others are labeled as ethnic or exotic. All cultures are of equal value and worth, the tribal is not inferior to the urban, the rural is not subordinate to the metropolitan. But those who have not been brought up in an ambience of cultural equality may be prompted by the greatness in political power or economic superiority to underestimate the real quality of cultures.

Unity, not uniformity, is the objective to be sought. Hence, diversity in unity, rather than unity in diversity, should be the goal of a new world. It is not just the goal depending upon any whimsical choice. But the facts of life are such that this world of ours is made up of many cultures. This plurality is a fact, and not a desideratum. Just as every language is adequate to meet the needs of its users, every culture is intrinsically on a par with other cultures, and it is in their reciprocal relationship that they jointly seek fulfillment. The hegemony of any single culture, like the hegemony of any single political power, will create an unhealthy atmosphere in which all cultures will ultimately perish. Together, they can flourish and replenish the earth, but when put in jeopardy by stressing globalization and ignoring regional creativity, they may prove sterile and stunted. Today, the threat is greater, since information technology seems to pave the path of standardization, until a counter-technology is developed which will control the tendency towards homogenization of cultures.

Marginalization can take place not only in the context of globalization; perhaps less conspicuous, but equally damaging can be the marginalization that takes place as a result of internal colonialism, without any external or extra-national force acting as a catalyst. The tribal people, the first nations, the aborigines are subtly bypassed, sidelined, and made marginal not only in the political sphere, but in the economic and cultural spheres too. The downtrodden communities in India, the Red Indians in America, the Innuits in Canada, the Maoris and Bushmen in Australia, the Afro-Americans in USA are living yet languishing examples of the tyranny of subjugation and subordination within the same country. The literature of every nation can sensitize each citizen to the deplorable situation arising from 'internal colonialism or the "imperial" display of power and hegemony maintained by one set of people over others within the same country. Perhaps this subjugation in subtle ways extends to the domestic sphere as well; the domination of the male over the female is a form of imposing male preferences on the female. Patriarchy of one kind or other is in operation in the imperial/colonial mode of human relationship. The impoverishment of culture resulting from the attempt at homogenization can be controlled and checked only if the existing power structure is not allowed to keep this imbalance.

The Indian term for 'culture' is 'sanskrti'. But if it is juxtaposed to *prakrti*, as in the dichotomy of nature versus nurture, it loses its vitality and validity, which are ultimately drawn from nature, human or non-human. It leads to the notion of dominance. It destroys the value of tolerance. Indian society is, and has always been, multiracial, multilingual, multi-religious, multiethnic, and so is the world today, and any attempt to reduce it to a mono-racial, mono-lingual, mono-religious, mono-ethnic will eventually lead to its ruin. The lotus flower is many-petalled, so are the rays of the sun, radiating in a wide spectrum and covering the entire multiverse, resplendent and glorious, magnificent and gorgeous in its immaculate splendour, displaying vibrant variety and rich diversity underlying its unity, celebrating the full orchestral symphony of diversity, resisting standardization, uniformity and homogeneity. Culture, *per se*, is resistance to tyranny, to centralization, to hegemony, to the domination of one over the many; it is *bahuvachan* or plural, by definition. In one sense there are only cultures: each nation is part of that map, contributing its specific flavour and savour. Culture is a mosaic, not a monolith. Culture is freedom, equality, recognition and acceptance of the other; it flourishes in an atmosphere of shared existence, a festival of differences and divergences, not a monochrome. True maturity or wisdom consists in imbibing the spirit of the other, without surrendering one's individuality and identity. The imposition of a hegemony we call imperialism; the surrender of autonomy we call colonialism. Neither imperial nor colonial is true culture. Let me end with a few lines from my poem called *Gotrayanam* (la migration of des tribus), describing the progress and proliferation of culture across man's history and the earth's geography:

Listen to me, friends,
  You, who have taken the pledge

To venture out, what is it
  That inspires us

To recreate the promised land?
Come, chiefs of the clans,
  Gautama, Kashyapa,

Vasishta, Parashara,
  Vishwamitra, Bharadwaja,
Leaders of the clans to be,
  Come, line up one by one,
  Those ready for the plunge.

Pack up in bundles
  The load we have to take:
The heritage we pride in,
  Ditties to be sung en route,
Fables and jokes
  To be listened to with joy;
Things to sustain us
  Through the long sojourn.

Refugees we are not,
  We wish not to plunder,

Neither buyers of land
  Nor sellers are we,
We are not merchants,
  We go as seekers, pilgrims.

Spurred on by the star
  That shines in fiery eyes,
We know and savour
  The depths of compassion,

We cancel and recast
  The calendar of wisdom;
Together we'll build
  A new edifice of culture.
The world we'll recognize
  As an ever-changing image,
And seek a foothold
  Along unfamiliar tracks.

To stay in one's own culture may be a virtue, but to outgrow one's own culture and recognize and accept other cultures is a greater glory, a greater fulfillment. So, let us proceed on this route of unending discoveries, infinite satisfactions and thrills. Vive la différence!

4

Premodern 'Superstitions'—A Counternormative Approach

M. Ramakrishnan

Introduction

The smooth and even contours that demarcate the modern from the premodern are the conceptual creations of modernity motivated by a deep-rooted myth rather than the logic of objective analysis. In the postmodernist view, the divide actually emerges from the modernist tendency to historicism propped on distinctly marked out binary opposites like man/nature, mind/matter, male/female and so on. The following table delineates the premodern/modern divide as conceived in different disciplines:

	Premodern	*Modern*
Economics	primitive	progressive
Positivist Psychology	superstitious savage	rational citizen
Theology	paganistic—heathenish	monistic—absolutistic

An extensive study of the conceptual distinctions stated above will, no doubt, show that the extremities of the boxes in the table are not so rigid as it is given, and the attributes are very often interpenetrating. In terms of modernist preferences, the interpenetration occurs only vertically and not at all horizontally.

It is not much relevant to ask whether the genes of modernity are Baconian or Cartesian as both the pioneers had asserted that mind as the locus of knowledge/thought is the testimony to genuine existence. The ensuing propositions equating knowledge with power (Bacon)/truth with clear and distinct ideas (Descartes) entail the assumed derogatory status of 'the myth loving and superstitious savage'. While taking this inferior status imposed upon the premodern for granted, none normally asks what the premodern would have thought of this rigid distinction and of the norms adopted for making it. This, at least with the reference to democratic values, which the modernist cannot do away with, is obviously unwarranted.

In the light of the emerging postmodernist critique of modernity, we are certainly in a position to develop and apply a set of *counternorms* to deconstruct the myth of modernity's self-image of its sham glory. Interestingly, this postmodernist venture to attack the vainglory of modernity has been initiated in the West itself. We cannot however forget the fact that the premodern/modern bifurcation had transcended its conceptual level to boost the morale of the colonial invaders from the West as it had been the case of America after Columbus had declared it discovered or that of India before independence.

The politicians, policy-makers and intelligentsia of India, if they cannot grasp and establish the fallacy of the premodern-modern divide, consciously or unconsciously commit themselves to the colonizers' logic of invasion and oppression. This is tantamount to our confession that all our premodern past is so worthless that we deserved and still deserve the domination of the modern, West. Unfortunately, the tendency to the indiscriminate acceptance of the modernist paradigms of development and cultural excellence is *pro rata* very high in India.

The Postmodernist Critique

There are two propositional options to rule out this self-defeating acceptance of the alleged worthlessness of our premodern traditions and the consequent commitment to Western domination.

(i) To prove that ours was not a premodern culture or

(ii) To prove that the premodern has its own intrinsic worth.

The first option is contrary to facts, and nevertheless it need not be maintained if the second one is true. So the focus of inquiry in this paper will be the prospects in working out a methodology to substantiate the second option stated above.

The *critical dimension* of such a methodology to inquire into the potential worth of the premodern is so much developed by postmodernist writers that we have many of the required tools in a ready-to-use condition. Hence, we have the concepts like anti-foundationism, rejection of meta-narratives, skepticism about the universal/global potentials of modernity and so on. Moreover, the emphasis on the incommensurability of cultures and belief-systems will be of much relevance in the normative reevaluation of the premodern. Before rereading our ancient traditions, both dead and living, one must be conscious of the consequences of the modernist vision of a "monolithic world in which everything is subsumed under a universal principle". (McGowan 1991: 13).

The crux of the postmodernist critique is that "the social totality within which we live is a *constructed* whole that gains unity only through a process of exclusion" (*ibid*.: 21-22). This leads to the creation of the *other*, which provides the dominator with the rationale for legitimizing his power over the other. Within the purview of this paper it is not easy and also not necessary to elaborate this critical dimension of a methodology to delineate the inherent values of the premodern as relevant materials are otherwise available in plenty.

Rereading the Premodern Texts

So we can pass on to the question what we, at the receiving end of modernity's sham glory, have to contribute to the inquiry into the unread value potentials of premodern cultures? The task is to diligently reread the texts of premodernity that include the various belief-systems, sense of the self, and institutions in relation to the respective communities that form their *terra firma*. Anyway, one should remember that heterogeneity is so pervasive in the premodern texts that we cannot be confident of a perusal.

Another hindrance that we have to get rid of while investigating the premodern is the long-drawn-out understanding of history as macrohistory. Feminists always frown at history as *His-story*. Then from the premodern's point of view, it is quite warranted to look at history as *Hi-story*. It is analogous to Hi-tech contrasted with alternative technologies. History as *Hi-story* necessarily entails the bifurcation between a *hypertext* and a *hypotext*, and the former is normally linked with the glorious and the latter with the ignoble. So the history that emerges in the course of rereading premodern traditions will be a mosaic composed of microscopic instances and other contextualized narrations synthesized or often sandwiched without recourse to universal paradigms and/or metanarratives. In the Indian context, it is a confusing mosaic of often distinguished and often interpenetrating units of tribal and rural culture.

Study of the premodern is always expected to result in histories rather than a history, and even the findings about a microlevel phenomenon, for instance, a festival or an agricultural practice, will the analyst further into an infinite array of subhistories. Macrohistorical method is bound by the *centripetal dynamics* of the components and hence it is practically incompatible with the study of a polycentric phenomenon like the premodern. This misapplication of macrohistorical method has been largely responsible for neglecting the *ecological continuity* in our premodern culture. An ecological history of India would have accommodated the otherwise diverse cultures of premodernity. Some pioneering works in this area have already appeared.[1] There are also works concentrating on local history with the ecological dimension in focus.[2] These works are in general marked by the advantages of synthesizing the insider approach with scientific method. This is essential for any analyst who wants to avoid the pitfalls of macrohistorical conditioning that may prompt him/her to look down on the premodern categories given. In the Indian context, the categories are composed mainly of the *gotracaras* or tribal conventions and *desacaras* or rural conventions.

The Tribal and Rural Streams

In any analysis of the Indian premodernity, we must necessarily take into account the *dialectical coefficients* of cultural transmission and cultural conflict pertaining to the tribal and rural streams. The elements of conflict can be substantiated with reference to their worship patterns. The unique feature of tribal social life is explained thus:

> (...) they impute sacred qualities to a number of landscape elements, plants and animals in their own immediate surroundings. Indeed their world is a community of beings: rocks, rivers, trees, birds and beasts with whom the humans are linked in a variety of ways.
>
> (Gadgil and Berkes 1991: 129(3))

Tribals perform rites normally in an open grove in the midst of wilderness with huge trees and thick greenery forming the backdrop. So the place of worship is an *unsystematized* whole that accommodates the trees, gods and the worshippers alike. It does not have a distinct walled structure or a distinct hierarchy regulating the worship. A festival or *puja* is just an occasion for community gathering in which all the members eat, sing and dance together. In short, the worship pattern as a whole is *open* and *even*, and it reflects the tribal worldview.

The rural tradition is distinctly marked by the presence of *gramaksetras* with well-arranged temple buildings.[3] The position of the sanctum sanctorum and subsidiary temples is as prescribed in a well-defined *vastu sastra*. There is a distinct priestly class privileged to enter the temples and to perform rituals. All non-Brahmin castes are allowed to worship the gods from outside the temple walls. It is all *structured* architecturally as well as socially. So the rules of social distance correspond to a caste's spatial distance from the divine points in a temple.

Notwithstanding the aforesaid distinction between the unstructured tribal worship pattern and the structured one in the rural tradition there are certain elements of cultural transmission between the two. It can be measured well in terms of *ecological continuity*. Hence the two distinct but interconnected streams of India's premodern tradition serve our purpose of explicating its inherent values in the form of a set of ecofriendly customs, beliefs, and practices. In order to analyze them in the proper perspective, neither a prejudiced view of the premodern as primitive nor a mere descriptive study will help.

The Transcendental Method

A better and more proper method of analysis should incorporate a *transcendental dimension* into the study. Hence it is necessary to go beyond what is given in order to seek the unread and even unintended dimensions of the actual text. This approach is to be stressed further in the light of the fact that the premodern units are characteristically unconcerned with a rationale to support any social custom. The transcendental analysis may focus either on some widely adopted belief systems or on some localized belief systems. The former is represented by the conceptual frameworks like the vision of nature as theophany or divine revelations (Versluis, 1992: 94) and the concept of nature as *mother goddess*, which is 'almost a universal phenomenon in primitive cultures' (Mahapatra, 1992, p. 65). Such widely adopted concepts have been elaborated in many works dealing with the social anthropology of primitive religions.[4]

The transcendental analysis of localized systems is more difficult as they are too many and too various to facilitate any kind of elaborate and exhaustive study; even so the nature and goal of this work permit and moreover necessitate the presentation of one or two instances in order to demonstrate the concealed worth of our premodern customs in terms of their ecological import.

(i) The socio-religious taboo on fishing in the temple ponds or *ciras* of Kerala is well known. This is to be linked with the absence of any such taboo on fishing beyond the temple premises. As the fishes in the *cira* adjoining the village shrine are left forever untouched, the prospect of their free breeding is ensured. As a result the whole system works as a natural hatchery of a variety of indigenous Pisces. This is indeed an otherwise unread positive value inherent in the 'superstition' that prompts the believers to maintain the *cira* as a sacred site. It is indeed an ecologically beneficial practice in terms of biodiversity conservation especially in these days of unruly predation of natural resources.

(ii) A desacara linked with the famous *Andalur Kavu* temple in Dharmadam Panchayat of Kannur district is noteworthy. Every temple in Kerala has a vivid backdrop of oral history relating the desacaras to some divine incarnation. Hence the *theyyarn*[5] performances in this *gramakshetra* are said to represent the *vanavasa* story in the *Ramayana*. The interesting fact about this kavu is that it is the only one in northern Kerala with the *theyyarn* performance of Rama and Lakshmana as we have in all other *gramakshetras* the performances representing only non-sanskritic gods. Among the set of rituals in *Andalur Kavu* we here focus on the one termed *chakka kothu*, which in a poor translation is the ritual of cutting the jackfruit in devotion to the *daivathar* who is the very incarnation of Lord Rama.

This ritual is followed by a strict *desacara* according to which the local people abstain from reaping and eating jackfruits, which is a domestic favorite of Keralites. This taboo is strictly observed for about four months from *thulam* 10th to *kumbham* 2nd, the day of the ritual. The venerable sources of oral history in the village relate this customary and seasonal taboo to the story of Rama's exile in the forest where the lord and his companions had to depend upon the fruits in the forest for subsistence. May be the villagers wanted to leave their fruits of great relish for the free use of their beloved gods.

By carefully reading the aforementioned custom, we can delineate an ecological finger post therein. The taboo on using the fruit is valid from *thulam* 10th *kumbham* 2nd which roughly corresponds to the period from mid-October to the end of February. Actually, this is the season for jackfruit trees to blossom and bear fruits. So the customary taboo that prompts the villagers to abstain from using the fruits will certainly let a large number of them withstand reaping, and as a result a sufficient number of jackfruit seeds will attain maturity for germination within the taboo period.

The significance of this unread and sometimes unintended dimension of the given taboo is to be understood in the light of the fact that jack fruit tree is considered to be the best suitable for making wooden support and furniture for houses. This makes jack fruit trees a much-sought out favourite of wood industry in Kerala and consequently, the trees are being cut indiscriminately.

In the preceding analysis of a few instances of localized customs, we have found only the tip of the iceberg; there are many other dimensions and yet still many other icebergs. Anyway, one thing that we have to note in this kind of transcendental analysis of premodern categories is the fact that each one of them is characteristically localized and therefore the analysis must be contextualized. So, an analyst requires not only a distancing from the macrohisorical canons and expectations but also a diligent insider involvement in the given text.

Postscript

One necessary conclusion derived either by means of scientific deduction or in the form of emotional presupposition is that the so-called superstitions of the premodern are not at all worthless. Many such customs have an intrinsic ecofriendly dimension, but only thing is that it must be re-evaluated in the light of the mounting environmental disasters around us. Then the emerging environmental ethics with its antimodern prescriptions like biodiversity conservation and biospherical egalitarianism will be supported and enriched by the premodern traditions all over the world. So, we listen again to Chief Seattle saying: *Every part of this soil is sacred in the estimation of my people*. And so every tradition of the premodern world is sacred and valuable.

Notes

1. A pioneering work is M. Gadgil and R. Guha, *The Fissured Land—An Ecological History of India* (Oxford University Press: New Delhi, 1992).

2. For instance see Kusum Misra Panigrahi, *Festivals of Biodiversity* (Navadanya: New Delhi, 1999).
3. E. Unnikrishnan, *The Sacred Groves of North Kerala* (Samskriti: Kannur, 1997) in Malayalam.
4. An elaborate study can be found in S. Jayashanker, *Temples of Kerala* (Directorate of Census Operations: Kerala, 1997).
5. For instance see Christopher Key Chappie and Mary Evelyn Tucker, eds. *Hinduism and Ecology* (OUP: New Delhi, 2001).

References

Gadgil, M. and Berkes, F. 1991. "Traditional Resource Management Systems" in *Resource Management and Optimization* 8 (3-4).

Mahapatra, S. 1992. "Invocation: Rites of Propitiation in Tribal Societies" in Geeti Sen, Ed., *Indigenous Vision—Peoples of India Attitude to the Environment*, New Delhi: Sage.

McGowan, J. 1991. *Postmodernism and Its Critics*, London: Cornell University Press.

Versluis, A. 1992. *Sacred Earth—The Spiritual Landscape of Native America*, Vermont: Inner Traditions International.

In addition to the works cited above, I have depended much on the narrations by many insiders representing the tribal and rural streams of Kerala culture.

5

Places Without Roadmaps: Significance of "Place" in the Postcolonial Discourse

M. Madusudhana Rao

In the post-colonial discourse, the simultaneous co-existence of place and language as a means of identity is at two levels; first, it becomes a "presence" in the writer's mind in creating the mood and guiding the narrative destiny of his fiction; second, it becomes a means of internalizing the self and place for personal satisfaction. As this is true in many writers of the 80's and beyond in the Indian novelists in English (such as Amitav Ghosh in his *Shadow Lines*, where Calcutta and to some extent, like Rushdie's Mumbai, becomes richly internalized symbol), Khushwant Singh's Delhi (in his *New Delhi*), Shashi Tharoor's demythicized world of Indraprastha (in his *The Great Indian Novel*) and in Upamanyu Chatterjee's fiction, Bapsi Siddhwa's Lahore and Bombay alike, and Rohinton Mistry's Bombay and Canada—all become richly enduring "migrant metaphors". In all these cases, in the post-Rushdie era, writers universalize "personal" description of the place, when they internalize their places—their imaginary homelands in their chosen linguistic metaphor. Here, language is the mode of internalizing the "place". As they vivify the place in language and metaphor, irony and apathy, endearment and disgust—finally the place "becomes" the poet's self.

In the case of Rushdie, all his historical/historyless destinations from Calf Island in Grimus to Chupland and Gupland are unique moments of "migrant metaphors", ultimately the writer's motif of displacement is possible in fleeting moments of linguistic dislocation. What is "place" in Rushdie? It is nothing but as language "experiences" it. Language stylizes the writer's self in his identity (in his unconscious level with a multiplicity of lands). Place is a phenomenological conception of the self and his experience is the suitable metaphor. Thus, "place" is not a geographical signifier of the writer's vagabondage in language.

In the case of Salman Rushdie, as in many postcolonial writers, writing contemporaneously, place is no longer a mere geographical entity as in the past, as in Narayan's Malgudi, Raja Rao's Kanthapura (however mythicised it may be, with all its Sthalapurana). In Rushdie, as in Amitav Ghosh, "places" are nothing but "suggestive" linguistic markers of the writer's imagination, ever so fleeting. Ultimately, "place" it is as exists in the writer's imagination. As "shadow lines" are "erased", they evoke "images" of writer's perception. Each "place" is stylized in various ways in the writer's imagination, as, in reality, they need not exist. What are apparent real-life monoliths (as Rushdie's Bombay with its humdrum and ambience, Ghosh's Kolkota with its Sunderbans setting), they are realized as highly personalized emotional spaces of the writers' imagination. Here, language is the medium of such a near poetic evocation. Thus, this paper has three parts: the first part discusses how the sense of "place" (vis-a-vis time) becomes the particular need of Rushdie in his fiction; second part discusses his stylistic devices in creating such poetic evocations of places, while the third part discusses how, ultimately, his novels become allegories of many places and times, as his goal is to evoke "imaginary home lands", emotively, unlimited by time and space.

Grimus is an imaginary ideal of scientific Utopia. Rushdie describes Calf Island Is bizarre, linguistic metaphors. He renders it in surrealistic detail. It was called Phoenix because it had risen from the ashes of a great city called Phoenix. Here, Rushdie is further mythicizing what is obviously a myth. It is a small town. Even its temporality is atemperal. Space is highly ethereal, the human "responses" and "consequences" of such a "place" are significant. As the narrative's intended purpose is "to locate" a timeless human consciousness, its consequences are in the realm of the impossible. Here, the "values" of the world are subverted. Here one will live long with an illness of the mind; one will bring grief and suffering to those whom they know. Here, the place is connated thus. There Death is "a blue fluid, blue like the sea, vanished down a monster's throat. Without the language of his ancestors for the archipelagoes of the world," Flapping Eagle drifted to Calf island. In a world of endless Phoenix myth of the Calf Island, Flapping Eagle lives for "a total of seven hundred and seventy-seven years, seven months and seven days". Calf Island is an "island of immortals", who found their longevity though unbearable and yet unwilling to give up. It has the likeness of self and mountain, of mist-isolated island and much-travelled continents.

Here, as according to Virgil Jones, are "analogies of human attributes and behaviour". For Flapping Eagle, "birds kingdom is remarkably suitable for myth makers". It has human parallel, with its own languages, courtship and female ties. As he describes many birds, "the profusion of bird-gods in Antiquity," Eagle is a symbol of the Destroyer in the Amerindian mythology. As the Gorfic planet is sometimes called Thera, it is found around the star Nus in the Yawy Klim galaxy of the Gorfic Nirveesu. The Gorfs look like "nothing so much as enormous sightless frogs" and made of rock.

In Midnight's Children place (vis-a-vis time) acquire even greater depth and purpose, than in Grimus. Here, like Time, Space is universalized. If in Rushdie, Time moves from temporal/historical to ahistorical eternity, place becomes a universal symbol of human drama. It is Mumbai, in particular, it is true—yet it is universal this drama could be everywhere—an archetype of provenance of human action. Here, in this narrativasition of human self in a holistic moment (of time and place), history may not be a mere background; it may be without any real life importance to the world of Saleem Sinai. For Rushdie, "memory truths" are more important than "literal truths". According to Ralph J. Crane, the relationship between the nation and self in this narrative is "a metaphor for the relationship between any human being and his world". Rushdie "chutnifies" history to "re-construct" (as it were) "our" history olfactorily, in deference to the history constructed by the Other. As he views history and place from this end (like all the postcolonial writers and thinkers, like Fanon), he believes that Eurocentric Other is incompatible with our life processes. He reverses 'Othering' by Orientalising (in Said's sense) our history and sense of place. Thus, place, like time, is a product of our sense of legitimacy and "authority". As we describe our sense of time in our attitude to history, place, too, has its own autonomy and pluralistic purpose. It is not a monolith, as construed by the Empire. Here, by re-employing new spatial designs, Rushdie is debunking all the derogatory metaphors of the Orient as an irredeemable "place" of depravity and inadequacy.

Thus, for Rushdie, time and space are not mere ectoplasmic methods to provide an erasable epidermal layer of history and place; nor does it. In any "vital" manner "touch" their lives. From the beginning, there are two histories or time and place realities: one is, Saleem and his birth, and the birth of other Midnight's Children. It is interesting to note that, right from their birth (on the midnight of August, 1947 till 1977 March), their lives are sought to be synchronized—though, in reality, it is the narrator's (could be author's) sense of history and place in a different mood, tone and purpose, from that of Saleem and Midnight's Children. As according to Frederick Jameson, in *Midnight's Children* and *Shame*, two novels of national allegories, there are two histories: one history of the nation and the other as history as olfactory memory. It may be possible to say, that the author's sense of time and place predetermine Saleem's temporal and spatial contours, as he becomes a living symbol of human self, being "chained to history". This symbolic deliverance of Saleem Sinai from 1947 to 1977 is through the atemporal means of final decimation of his self. Thus, in all these cases, the narrator's sense of history and place have a far reaching significance. For Rushdie, his interest is in imagining near deathless metaphors of time and place. For him, time and place provide poetic spaces for imagining newer places and times. This is his aspiration and continuous 'motifs' in which the lives of Saleem, Grimus and others are possibilities of externalizing such a poetic longing. As thus his goal is strictly a "personal" emotional need, his true sense of time and place are mostly his sensory dreams of any time and any place.

In all these cases, it is ultimately through the innovative use of style that he "describes" himself. Here, style appears similar in their tone, syntax and lexicon. Rushdie stylistically evokes the world of material actuality with the world of fantasy. If one serves a narrative/topical end, the other is, indeed, his personal need. If one uses near referential language, the other uses the highly emotive near pseudo-statements of (I.A. Richards) with the polytonal associations of "suggestions". If the first one helps in rendering the prosaic situation (of historical actuality), the other wins our attention to give us joy.

Stylistically, as Rushdie employs a two-prong mode, a prosaic and poetic mode, ultimately, it is in his poetic rendering of his imaginative, dreaming self of place that acquires maximum significance. In the prosaic mode, language is intentionally factual and unemotional, bordering on near documentary evidence. Facts, not "effects" matter here. Here, Bombay is eked out in unemotional, factual detail. It could be called "landscape" of a typical urban setting:

> And fishermen and Catherine of Braganza and Mumbaaasevi coconuts rice; Sivaji's stature and Methwold's Estate; a swimming pool in the shape of British India and a two-storey hillock; a centre-parting and a nose from Bergerac; an imperative clock-tower and a little circus ring;
>
> (*Midsummer Children*, p. 126)

Here, the verbs evoke action of concrete nouns of "swimming pool, clock tower, circus ring". And in another setting, the style is racy:

> We headed north, past Breach Candy Hospital and Mahalaxmi Temple, north along Hornby Vellard post Vallabhai Patel Stadium and Haji Ali's island tomb, north of what had once been...the island of Bombay. We were heading towards the anonymous mass of tenements and fishing-villages and textile-plants become in these

> northern zones...(Not at all far from where I sit within view of local trains!)

Here, even as the syntax is long and purposefully convoluted, and lexicon is referential, this description has, at the back of it, a creative voice of the narrator, to make them animate images of places, but not disinterested verbal hoardings.

In contrast, the near lyrical strain pervades in the vivacious use of language. Here, place is vivified in recurrent images:

> Midnight's Children!... From Kerala, a boy who had the ability of stepping into mirrors and re-emerging through any reflective surface in the land—through lakes and...the polished metal bodies of automobiles... and a Goanese girl with the gift of multiplying fish...and children with powers of transformation: a where wolf from the Nilgiri Hills, and from the great watershed of the Vindhyas, a boy who could increase or reduce his size at will, and had already been the cause of wild panic and rumours of the return of Giants.... From Kashmir, where was a blue-eyed child of whose sex I was never certain.... Some of us called this child Narada, others Markandaya,...

Here, as the language is evocative, lexicon carries with it the colour and landscape of the narrator's imaginative mind: words like, "reflecting surface in the land, the great watershed of Vindhyas and the "blue-eyed child" and Narada and Markandaya—all appeal to the timeless sense myth and imagination. In antoher case, the world of legendary Caliph Haroon al-Rashid is evoked. In a similar way, Saleem Sinai, the self-styled expatriate in his own country, travels in secrecy through by lanes of Mumbai, while on another occasion, Rushdie consciously mingles grim realism with an element of colour and splendour. Though this image may not have the ethereal quality of Narada and Markandaya, it is of the same kind:

> I have not shown you the factory in day light until now. This is what has remained undescribed: through green-tinged glass windows, my room looks out on to an iron catwalk and then down to the cooking-floor...

> In day light, our saffron-and-green neon goddess does not dance above the factory doors ... Human flies hang in thick white-troused clusters from the trains.
>
> (*Midnight's Children,* p. 251)

On another occasion, Rushdie's typical sardonic humour is at a slight angle between reality and fantasy though in fact, it is an aspect of the writer's "personal" judgement: Bombay for him is "a glamorous leech". It is "really a mouth, always hungry and swallowing food and talent from everywhere else in India".

Stylistically, the world of fantasy and reality in conjunction is realized in a splash of advertisement labels, "Kemp's corner, past Thomas Kemp and Co, beneath the Air-India rajah's poster...the Kolynos kid, a gleam toothed pixie in a green elfin, chlorophyll hat proclaimed the virtues of Kolynos Toothpaste (MC, pp. 181-82)—where the images themselves are inflated by Rushdie's "thyroid balloon of child with hair already sprouting tuftily on his lip". The significance of the place also carries with it the political and cultural context. It is a conscious contrast. Mumbai and Karachi are like two "sister-ships". Karachi is set between the desert and bleaky saline creeks, whose shores were littered with stunted mangroves. (Saleem's), new city seemed to possess an ugliness which "eclipsed his own city (Mumbai)". At the heart of his Karachi was Ali Aziz's house, "a place of shadows and yellowed paint." There in Karachi, "oases shone in the tarmac of Elphinstone street". "Umblical Cord" is the holistic metaphor connecting his poetic imagination. It was "implanted in the earth". It grew out of his poetic self to relate himself to the sub-continental psyche. Though physically drainage drained his inner life, his sense of "connection remained undrained". He sailed to Karachi by the south-east with his "hypersensitive nose". Finally, his retreat into India is mythicized in his vegabondage of places. He returned to India like Caliph Haroun—al-Rashid, "unseen, invisible, anonymous, cloaked through the streets of Baghdad". He, thus, "flew through the air-lanes of the sub-continent".

In all these willing dislocation of places—for whatever may be the purpose (identifying oneself with the sub-continent could be one of the purposes), Rushdie, the narrator-protagonist is conscious of the method of his imagination. For him, "matter of fact descriptions of the outre and bizarre" are not in so insignificant as "the stylized versions of the every day...(which are) attitudes of mind" form the kerb of his poetic purpose in evoking the spirit and "intended" need. To this extent, all places and even their names do not have any meaning and they are "still more than mere sounds". The modern men, like Rushdie, are "the victims of the titles". For example, "Sinai contains Ibu Sina, master magician, Sufi adept; and also sin the moon, the ancient god of Hadhramaut, ... sin is also the letters as sinuous as a snake.... Sinai when in Roman script the name of place-of-revelation (*Midnight's Children*, pp. 364-365).

To this extent, his sense of place is through Olfactory perception. He seeks "nasal freedom" of places. He believes in "the spectrum of fragrances" and "nasal inheritance". Sunderbans is "the forest of illusions". The Rann of Kutch is "a chamelon area" and "amphibian terrain, which was land for half the year and sea for the other half." The boatman Tais words also evoke the same world of "magic realism" of the place, where "Adam baba is just under the water's skin".

Stylistically, Shame employs more fantastic devices than Midnight's Children. Here, unlike in *Midnight's Children*, place is realized in surrealistic detail. If in the case of Midnight's Children, there is a tantalizing balance between the concrete and the suggestive evocation, here in Shame, the syntax and lexicon most obviously tilt towards the realms of the surreal:

> In the remote border town of Q, which when seen from the air, resembles nothing so much as an ill-proportioned dumb-bell, there once lived three lovely, and loving sisters.
>
> (*Shame*, p. 11)

Subversion (linguistic, most particular, though) is the predominant quality here:

> Omar Khayyam Shakil was afflicted, from his earliest days, by a sense of inversion, of a world turned upside-

> down ... he was living at the edge of the world, so close that he might fall off at any moment.
>
> (*Shame*, p. 21)

There are twin eternities of Omar Khayyam. Even the political identity (leave alone the geographical identity), is deliberately left to be mysterious. According to him, as there are two countries, one real and another fictional, his story and fictional country exist "at a slight angle to reality". 'Q' is not Quetta. He will call it Karachi, and it will contain a 'Defence'. Like Saleem, he is "a transplanted man", borne across the countries and like all migrants, he also leaves history behind. In a mood of exaggerated dislocation, Rushdie tells us, that "a city is a camp for refugees". He, like all migrants, "build(s) imaginary countries and try to impose them on the ones that exist". In a revealing metaphor, he tells us that he is like "the ash of Yggalrasil, the mythical world-tree of Norse legend." As the ash of Yggalrasil "will fall and darkness will descend, the twilight of the gods" would come, completing "a tree's dream of death". Thus, 'Q' real or imaginary, is at "a slight angle of reality".

In a similar way (though to a lesser extent), Chupland and Gupland of Haroun and Sea of Stories are highly stylized, even romanticized places of poet's imagination. With their dystopic purposes, they are not meant to be real at all. They are deliberately subverted projections of the writer's unconscious desire for freedom. As freedom is denied to the writer's self, he glorifies the lack of it, in powerful, subverted detail, only to create a world of grotesque in our minds.

Here, the lexicon is meant to be strange and even unusual. Even their semantic or linguistic meanings are unusual. Each word has its autonomy of meaning and significance. It is an unusual language for an unusual experience:

> The Moon, Kahani travels so fast...that no Earth instruments can detect it; also its orbits varies by one degree per circuit, so that in three hundred sixty orbits it has overflown every spot upon the Earth.
>
> (*Haroun and Sea of Stories*, p. 67)

The land of the Guppy has Water Genie, process too complicated to Explain (PZz CZz) and "Thought Beams and Advanced Technology". There is a story telling machine. Gup City is imaginatively stationed, both in its astronomical and geological setting, between the Sun Kahani, Earth's second Moon. The Moon "travels so far that no Earth instruments can detect it." Its "orbit varies one degree per circuit so that in three hundred and sixty orbits it has overflown every spot upon the Earth.

Rushdie's recent venture, *Moor's Last Sigh* combines unmistakable fact, sensitized by personal detail. Here, it is not fantasy, in any case, but the geographical and historical reality that is internalized, with a sensory delight:

> Pepper it was that brought Vasco da Gama's tall ships across the ocean, from Lisbon's Tower of Belern to the Malabar Coast; first, to Calicut and later, for its lagoony harbour, to Cochin. English and French sailed in the wake of that first-arrived Portugese, so that in the period called Discovery of India but how could we be discovered when we were not covered before?
>
> (*Moor's Last Sigh*, p. 4)

Here, history and place are mostly in the realms of realism, though, as always with Rushdie, they are personalized tales of a family saga. The description of place in this case is, by and large, similar to near concrete rendering of Mumbai in *Midnight's Children*, though in this case, the lexicon is 'coloured' with a little more sensory detail. In any case, here, it is history of place in nearly exact and even identifiable, though it is delightfully sensory.

Thus, Rushdie achieves his universal concept of place through stylistic means. As for him, "imaginary homelands" are the true places of the human values of tolerance, and catholicity of purpose, he creates at multiple foci, at a tangential angle from reality these "migrant metaphors". He seeks "alternative realities" of existence in the contemporary nomadic self of the modern man. As these alternative realities create "a new heritage" of man, futuristically, Grimus's Calf Island at one level, is a futuristic possibility of man's eternal progress into a newer life of prophesy. This newly evolving universal and eclectic heritage of the modern writers (like Rushdie, who are 'translated men') gains in its evoking people realities, where for Rushdie, as "art is a passion of the mind, imagination works best when it is most free". In this "cultural and political history" of seeking newer lands of one's choice and values, his creative attitude defines itself. It is to acquire a liberation of his soul and creative art, uncluttered by the limitations of a particular place or time. As the pangs of being unrelated to any place themselves cause enough anguish, he, on the whole, is happy in being liberated and eclectic in time and space. It is this fruitful tension of being "displaced" and dispossessed of time and space, yet related to his "sense" of place with its own self-actualising temporal and spatial contours that provides the defining focus of his fictional imagination. As this displacement (or even migration) is rendered through his stylistic imagination, ultimately, it is this essential "sense" of language that creates his "imaginary lands". By fully exploiting language by various stylistic devices (as subversion, irony and paradox as the mainstay), he views migration as one complete metaphor to describe the metropolitan culture, be it Bombay. 'Q' or K. As, for the twentieth century man and writer, every act of progress involves a certain level of mobility and migration, Joyce's Dublin or Marquez's Macando, Rushdie's Bombay and Amitav Ghosh's Calcutta or Dhaka are all "shadow lines" of the memories of these poet-narrators in their fictions. Though the process of migration for Rushdie's protagonists is by means of intellectual activity and by conscious choice of priorities, for Rushdie, the writer, a vibrant linguistic medium creates the medium of imagination (for immense "personal" satisfaction) for weaving wonderful (or even dark in shame) newer lands. If migration is the universal need for his protagonists, imagining newer lands by deconstructing language and by endlessly rich semantic variety of connotation and denotation, creates immense joy for Rushdie, the author-narrator in all his narratives, as it also fulfils his creative need. As according to D.E. Maxwell, these postcolonial writers aim to "subdue the experience to the language the exotic life to the imported tongue." Thus, in the case of these postcolonial writers, it is the language which creates space. Fundamentally, their language (acquired/nativised english) is the main medium of their 'place'. For this purpose, writers like Rushdie, by using their own variety of english/English, unlimited by any circumstance or setting—be it fantasy/surrealistic, create their new 'place' as their medium makes it possible. To this extent, what is 'place' in Rushdie, is nothing but as his english/English describes it! By doing so, postcolonial writers like Rushdie, not only are "writing back to the centre", but even going further, as in the case of Soyinka, each "expression" by them creates its own "centre", thus dismantling the idea of 'centre' and 'periphery' in the present level of debate of post-colonial theory. Rushdie's Calf Island or Mumbai is as autonomous and significant in defining our culture, as Dickens's and Virginia Woolf's London or Jane Austen's Hampshire. By their essential leap, these postcolonial writers are "universal", as their places are without road maps or their works are not political allegories. Their language facilitates their universal entourage. It is the autonomy of the self through autonomy of language that is the achievement of Rushdie, the man and the writer.

References

Frederick Jameson, "Third World Literature in the Era of Multinational Capitalism." *Social Text*, Vol. 15, 1986, pp. 65-88.

Rushdie, *Imaginary Homelands' Essays and Criticism*, London: Granta Books, 1991.

D.E. Maxwell as quoted in D.E. Maxwell in *Empire Writes Back*. ed. B. Ashcroff *et al.*

6

Voices Behind the Veil: Representing Bhakti

Usha V.T.

Any effort to deconstruct/reconstruct women's discourse from the historical past would perforce bring up questions regarding methodology and frames of reference. Indeed the ways in which culture is constructed would also come to be scrutinized. Issues such as the authenticity of the woman's voice and the socio-cultural framework of the utterance would also of necessity surface. Many questions such as: "What is women's discourse?" "Would it exclude men, or would there be space for "the sympathetic male"? "Is there a female nature?" crop up repeatedly. Which feminist theory, or what feminist tools would enable one to deconstruct and then reconstruct women's discourse from the past and study their relevance in the present context?

A cursory survey of the field of feminist aesthetics would bring into focus two divergent perspectives towards studies relating to women: 1. Gynesis and 2. Gender theory. Of these Gynesis foregrounds the biological aspects of womanhood in any woman centered analysis. French feminists like Helence Cixous (1976, 1986) and Luce Irigaray (1991) place much emphasis on the physical aspects of women's writing and attribute it to female bodily expressions. They see fragmented discourse with space for gaps and disruptions as essential characteristics of women's discourse. They regard heteroglossic voices and multiplex diction as well as a tendency to be cumulative or repetitive and the tendency to employ metaphors of fluidity as essential to women's discourse. The repeated use of the continuous present as well as the taking up of a decentering point of view is considered another hallmark of woman's writing. (Such a linguistics state would automatically preclude men from women's studies) Greater emphasis of subjectivity and personalized narration in women's language as opposed to abstract and objective ways of expression would automatically deny the place of scientism and a systematic approach from the field of women's studies in general. Gynesis would in a sense lead to a certain amount of ghettoism and exclusivity with regard to anything related to women.

Gender theory on the other hand, is quite in opposition to such a purely womanish approach. It takes in to account socio-religious and cultural bias in the construction of gender attitudes. From the generalizations that encompass all women, it moves toward theories that treat women in individual terms and focus on the individual acted upon by multiple socio-religious and cultural factors that actually constitute frames of reference for us. Gender theory denies that there is a female nature. Marilyn French, feminist aesthetician, in an essay entitled, "Is there a Feminist Aesthetics?" describes feminist art thus:

> First it approaches reality from a feminist perspective: second, it endorses female experience. The feminist perspective is partly a Reversal of patriarchal views...(it focuses on people as a whole...as part of a community. (*Aesthetics in Feminist Perspectives*. Ed. Hilda Hein and Carolyn Korsmeyer. Bloomington, Ind. 1993, pp. 153-65.)

For the purposes of this paper, I intend to be eclectic and draw from these two antithetical approaches drawing from both positions to raise interesting questions that bring up representations from the medieval period thereby attempting to create and maintain a synthesis.

In the context of this theoretical framework, I enter into my discussion about the poetics of Bhakti (devotion) in women's discourse. Is there a woman's voice there? What are the socio-cultural factors that led to the woman's religious experience? Did the woman find a voice there? If so, was it a purely woman's voice? Were there any common grounds through which the discourse of Bhakti included woman's experience? In order to foreground the woman's voice and the general features that bind the common woman's experience in spirituality, I look into the religio-mystical experiences of two south Indian women mystics of the medieval period through their poetics outbursts.

The writing of history as we know, it has been primarily male-centred and excluded women automatically from the focus of attention. In a cultural framework where the woman's activity was constantly undervalued and devalued, and her presence ignored marginalized and unnoticed, such lack of mention could only be inevitable and in the natural scheme of things. As Jay Kleinberg in her introduction to *Retrieving Woman's History*, describes the process:

> Historians searching for evidence about women's history have encountered the phenomenon of women's invisibility; women have been systematically omitted from accounts of the past. This has distorted the way we view the past; indeed it warps history by making it seem as though only men have participated in events thought worthy of preservation and by misrepresenting what actually happened.
>
> (*Retrieving Women's History: Changing Perceptions of the Role of Women in Politics and Society*. Ed. S. Jay Kleinberg. Paris: UNESCO press, 1988)

This veil of invisibility has kept aside perspectives that privilege women as well as women centred narratives from the mainstream of socio-political and religio-cultural discourse. Any attempt to recreate women's history or uncover hitherto invisible/hidden documents thereby assumes a certain revolutionary zeal. Susie Tharu and K. Lalitha record a similar experience in their efforts to locate and collate women's writing in India. In their preface to their pioneering work *Women Writing in India*, they make specific mention of the problems in unearthing women's discourse and disentangling it from male centred literary history.

> We read against the grain of literary histories taking special note of writers who were criticized or spoken about dismissively, or controversies that involved women. Social histories biographies and autobiographies we found often provided information that literary histories had censored.
>
> (*Women Writing in India,* 1993)

This tendency to devalue women centric perspectives or neglect them totally is merely one means of marginalizing the female voice. Another effective method of silencing the woman was the socio-cultural approach valorising silence as a desirable feminine trait. This consciously evolved tactic denied speech or expression to the "good woman", privileging the male entirely. Women were not expected to have an opinion at all. She was only expected to act in servile silence. If at all she did have an opinion, the well brought up woman was not expected to articulate it—particularly in public spaces or social gathering where she could be heard. An "opinionated" was usually treated with a certain amount of distaste and women who continued to express themselves despite social disapproval would be christened as shrews gossips or chatterboxes and represented as objects of ridicule and social ostracism. Only the silent, sweet-natured, caring the submissive (read servile) woman could be foregrounded as part of the mainstream culture.

While much of the world slipped easily into these stereotypical notions of woman in the socio-religious context, India could boast of a uniquely woman centred religious outlook as part of its mainstream. The female deity was worshipped as Devi as well as the mother goddess, the Life giving force, a source of immense power and energy. The ideal of the goddess as shakthi, the vital power was venerated. She was the epitome of peace, plenitude and harmony in her various *avatars* as Devi, Lakshmi, Amma/Ambal and Saraswathi. She was also the violent, avenging and awesome Kali, the destroyer of evil and the preserver of justice. Both the harmonious and the violent aspects of the feminine were equally respected and worshipped. She was venerated in equal terms with the male principle and the concept of Ardhanareeswara where the male and female principles were fused together in equal measure was part of the popular psyche.

This preoccupation with the cult of the goddess remains strong even in present day India. But the veneration of female principle has not been translated into the prevalent socio-cultural values with regard to women, despite the religio-spiritual thrust. Elinor Gadon, the American researcher into women's spirituality, has recorded the process by which the goddess in most religious cultures has lost her value.

> As history was written by the victors, goddess religion has been portrayed as heretical, bad, "of the devil", the alien other. Woman, identified with the goddess and her ways were also so branded and denied full participation in society. The transition was not just a gender change from goddess to god but a paradigm shift with the imposition of a different reality of different categories of being that deeply affected every human relationship. Woman, the female, the feminine, was excluded in this shift of consciousness. All that was most valued in the goddess culture, was revalued, given lesser priority, rejected.
>
> (Gadon, E. *The Once and Future Goddess: A Symbol of Our Time*, New York: Harper Collins, 1989)

Such a paradigm shift has not occurred within the religious cultural space of India in terms of the goddess. But the woman as the female or the feminine principle in socio-domestic terms has come to be devalued and suffered rejection on many grounds in the socio-cultural space. The contradiction though irrational is clearly true, and a study of the woman mystic would perhaps provide us with answers to the inevitable questions that arise out of the situation.

The religious sphere was one area where woman's work and participation received not only social sanction but active encouragement. From a very early age socio-cultural pressures encouraged women to be devout and display religious fervour. In their personal lives and the domestic scene as well as in the larger religio-cultural frame where their active involvement was required, women were expected to be participants. Many women who were otherwise marginalized as social rejects found acceptance and solace through religious involvement. Yet the question that recurrently comes up is—was it unconditional acceptance. Yet, closer analysis reveals that even expression through *bhakti* gained acceptance only when the women concerned worked within the guidelines prescribed by a watchful patriarchy. When women found voice beyond the accepted canons their spirituality was immediately treated as deviant or they were raised into an idealized state beyond the range of the average woman. In Europe, they were either burned at stake or (even later) canonized. But what was the situation in India? Let us examine through an analysis of the medieval period which experienced much religious revivalism.

The Bhakti revival in south India spreading over several centuries from the 6th to the 16th, like its counterpart in the rest of India foregrounded the common folk practices over the rigid and the classical. It broke across the rigid class structures and socio-religious conventions and gathered within its fold several of the subaltern peoples such as the lower castes and women of all castes and classes. By structure revolutionary and revivalist at the same time, the Bhakti movement gained popular support and remained in the mainstay of the popular imagination for a long time to come. Designed as a protest against the upper class hegemonial order in religion through codified religious practices, rituals and scriptures, the movement gained much of its widespread following through orally constructed discourse. Hence it could be related to the Desi, or the Bhasha tradition rather than to the classical Sanskritic Marga tradition. The songs and vacanas were composed and "written" in the regional language as opposed to Sanskrit, thereby assuming greater access to the masses often untutored and unlettered. However, this wealth of literature shows the synthesis of Vedic, Puranic and Agamic (or Tantric) elements containing theological concepts, mythologies and religious observances with practices and beliefs arising indigenously in the region. Perhaps we could also read in these the fusion of the two cultural streams from the regional and the Sanksritic, reflecting the amalgamation of cultures that must have taken place centuries earlier. Of course, the major thrust of the Bhakti narrative was towards the popularization of the once canonical.

One of the major factors that contributed to its profound success was the intensity of emotion and extremely personalized nature of its spiritual content. The Bhakti Movement and more specifically the Bhakti poetry while deeply religious and devotional, had a very physical and earthy aspect as well. Though celebratory and devotional, the poems reveal a very physical and sensual relationship between the bhakta and his/her Lord. Cultural historians like Friedhelm Hardy have drawn attention to the physical aspect of their poetry when the describes the poetry of the Alwars as "a highly sensuous and sensual world of human experience," thereby foregrounding the markedly erotic quality of their poetry (Hardy, F. *The Religious Culture of India: Power, Love and Wisdom*, Cambridge University Press, 1995, p. 523). Though both male and female mystics brought in the physical and included the sensuous descriptions of the body, it is in the poetry of the women mystics that the sensuousness reaches the peak of its emotional intensity.

Andal was the only woman among the Alwars, 12 in number, were devotees of Vishnu, who lived in the Tamil country of South India between the 6th and 10th centuries. The movement produced in its wake a large collection of songs in Tamil which earned for Hinduism a widespread following that stayed powerful for a long time. Andal's songs the *Tiruppavai*, running to 30 verses and the lesser known *Nacciyar Tirumoli*, a set of fourteen rhymes in 143 verses form part of the larger Alwar collection, called the *Nalayira Divyaprabhandam* (Four Thousand Divine Treatises).

Andal's *Tiruppavai* is sung even today especially by young unmarried girls during the Tamil month of Margazhi (December/ January) with the belief that it will bring them an early happy marriage. The Pavai vow undertaken by the maidens throughout the month required that they bathed at dawn in the chilly waters of a river or pond. While Manikkavacakar's Tiruvapavai (another religio-mystical poem on the same theme) describes the girls frolicking in the water Andal's poem limits itself to the waking up of the Lord in preparation of the ritual. Andal who is also the protagonist of the songs and her *sakis* (companion) go to Krishna's home and call upon his parents Nandagopal and Yasoda, his brother Baladeva as well as his cowherd wife Nappinnai to awaken him. The maidens then plead with Krishna "to bathe us now in the waters". The term *neeratal* or bathing can be interpreted at several levels. The purifying ritual of the bathing could be equated to the spiritual cleansing experienced by a *bhakta* (devotee) of diving deep into her Lord. Here, the meaning of the term Alwar translated as 'one who dives deep (into the divine)' brings into the poems a deeper signification. And the absence of the actual bath in the poems gives greater vehemence to this interpretation. Both Vidya Dehejia, translator and art historian, as well as Dennis Hudson interpret the terms *neeratal* (bathing in the water) and *cunaiatal* (bathing in hilltank) as euphemisms for sexual union. According to Hudson, the goal of the maidens is

> Intimate service to Krishna, which may mean sexual union with him euphemistically referred to as a bath: 'bathing in Krishna', one may say is the goal—a relationship of service so total that there are no limitations whatsoever.
>
> (Hudson, Dennis, "Bathing in Krishna: A Study of Vaishnava Hindu Theology". *Harvard Theological Review*, 73, 1980, p. 5555)

The sensuousness and the overtly sexual descriptions in the poem reinforce such interpretations. The descriptions of Napinnai in Stanzas 18 and 20 are directly sensual:

And maiden Nappinai with breasts
Tender and cup-like, red mouth, small waist,
Goddess of Beauty and fortune .... (St 20)

Your fingers so dexterous with the ball,
Red lotus hands with jingling bangles—(St 18)

The sensual expressions, through contrary to popular perceptions of religious discourse, nevertheless gave expression to a greater intensity of feeling. *Naacciyar Tirumoli*, the song of bridal mysticism is replete with the corporeal images of her love for her Lord for she sings

> Know, Manmatha, I will not live
> If my broad breasts, set apart
> For that great God with discus and conch
> Are bandied as meant for man
> .... St 4 P. 29

She sees her female body, her femaleness, as a reason for celebration, her beauty as a means to her goal and marriage or sexual union as one of the methods of reaching it. Such utterances in our own time would be termed womanist or feminist, yet perhaps fail to adhere to the depths of emotional fervour attained by the songs of Andal.

The context of Tiruppavai has Andal and her sakis pleading with Nappinai Krishna's wife to wake up the Lord, and part with Him for a short while in order to allow them to fulfil their Pavai vow. The 30 verses of Tiruppavai are full of admiring physical descriptions of the Lord, the epitome of manhood, his handsome physical self, his heritage, his exploits as cowherd, protector of the helpless, vanquisher of evil as king and as mischievous lover. The repetitive use of the refrain *Ellorambave*, contributes much to the continuity as well as the musical quality of the poem, reminding us everytime of the pavai vow in which context it was written. Yet, the ritual is treated in sensual terms rather than the purely metaphysical and through this air of aesthesis, spirituality is achieved.

The subdued physicality and the sexual suggestions seen in these poems become more overt and insistent as she moves towards the next set of poems, the Nacciyar Tirumoli. The tone becomes more personal and intimate and the emotional fervour is deeply intense and passionate. The poet-mystic is direct and frank in her outcry of physical longing for her divine lover, as she calls upon him to "fulfill my womanhood". The sakis and others recede into insignificance as the songs develop and become the expression of the individuals solitary plea for union with her divine lover—a highly personalized expression of her devotion.

Perhaps it is the violent emotions the repeated references to the pain of separation and the use of explicit sexual imagery that has made this set of poems less popular in common religious usage in comparison to her other poem Tiruuppavai, which is ritually and devotionally sung in the temples even today. In fact only the sixth song of the Nacciyar Tirumoli starting with the phrase "Varanamayiram" is recited at Vaisnava weddings in South India for its devotional quality in bridal mysticism. This section contains a gloriously detailed description of the Nacciyar's dream in which she finally weds her Divine Lord. The ceremony with all the rituals preceding the nuptials is described in elaborate detail, beginning with a procession of elephants moving through the ritual bath and purification, the ceremonial welcome, the chanting of vedic mantras and the traditional wedding rituals. None of the physical and conventional features of a traditional marriage are denied in this projected vision of the bhakta's union with the divine in an ecstasy of religious mysticism.

Thus the mysticism of the medieval period had a revolutionary quality by means of which it could give voice and include within its fold several of the people marginalized by the conventional society of the period. Women of all castes and classes, those considered socially insignificant and thus far inferior castes came to be foregrounded in this system and gained social acceptance. Yet, this is not to state that the social acceptance came without any opposition. Here one has to take into account legends and oral descriptions handed down through the generations as legitimate historical proof of their having existed.

Hagiographical accounts describe Andal's adoption by Vishnuchitta or Perialwar, one of the prominent Alwar saints in the first half of the 9th century. The *Srivilliputtur Sthala Purana* describes the birth of the goddess Bhudevi on earth as fulfilment of her desire to experience the bliss of divine longing in an earthly body. The divine child was found by Vishnuchitta, a priest at the temple amidst the sacred tulasi bushes around his home. Naming the child Kotai, Vishnuchitta raised her as his own daughter, tutoring her in the tradition of devotion and mysticism. From a very early age, Kotai or Andal saw herself as the bride of the God she worshipped and completely rejected the notion of an earthly lover. She adorned herself with flowers meant for the deity and spent hours pining for and awaiting her divine consort. Here, she came in for much earthly chastisement, even from her adoring father as wearing or even trying on the flowers kept aside for worship of the deity would amount to sacrilege. Consequently, Vishnu is said to have appeared to Perialwar in a dream and announced that the garland worn by Andal was especially dear to him. Henceforth, the first *puja* at the temple at Srivilliputtur, performed at dawn involves the transference of the garland worn by Andal the previous day or to the reigning deity Vishnu. This extraordinary ritual, which continues even today goes contrary to all traditional sastric conventions. What would have been considered polluting under traditional parameters, is under this system of Bhakti treated as acceptable and even lauded and the protagonist of the legend was given a new name *cuti-kotuha-nacciyar*. Yet, before she gains acceptability in the conventional sense, she has to undergo much social ostracism.

Similar social ostracism is recorded by hagiographical accounts on the Virashaiva saint Mahadeviakka as well, the severity of the disapproval recorded through the oral discourse of her poetry.

Virasaivism or the Lingayat Movement was a twelfth century Bhakti revivalist movement in the land of the Kannadigas—now Karnataka. Inverting the traditional paradigms of power, the Virasaivites reached amazing mystical heights and were able to restructure the society of their time. Their advent marked a turning point in the social spheres. Their presence brought down caste barriers, as well as gender and class distinctions. The Lingayat saints which included Prabhudeva, Akka Mahadevi, Basavanna, Allamma Prabhu, and Cenna Kesava, along with their followers and disciples on the path of the spiritual quest constituted themselves into an assembly called the Anubhava Mantapa, or the hall of Mystical Experience where they held their dialogues or discussions of a religious or mystical nature. Their discussions primarily of an oral nature have been collected and recorded by their followers in two great works—the *Prabhulinglile* and the *Sunyasampadane,* and their individual poems have been handed down to us as the *vacanas*, the poets themselves being called the *vacanakaras*. (The very term vacanakara is a derivative of vacana, prioritizing the *vacanas*). The idea of gender discrimination and inequality was challenged by their spokespersons. Both the male and female mystics rejected the conventional approaches to gender. In a vacana, Goggave, a woman *vacanakara* says:

> They call one a woman if one has breasts and a braid; they call one a man if one possesses moustache and a loincloth. Is knowledge of these twain Male or Female? O Nasthinatha.
>
> (Goggave 6, in Hiremath 1968, 185)

Similar sentiments are expressed by the male vacanakaras as well. For instance, Jadara Dasimayya disregards both gender and class as part of his spiritual quest. In a vacana he critiques contemporary society thus:

> Did the breath of the mistress
> have breasts and long hair?
> Or did the master's breath
> wear the sacred thread?
> Did the outcaste, last in line,
> hold with his outgrowing breath the stick of his tribe?
>
> (Ramanujan, 1973)

To him, breath signifies the living soul of the *bhakta* which cannot be classified in terms of class, caste or gender. In the Virasaiva scheme, they sought to do away with the notion of pollution, one of the major means of marginalisation. By doing so, they could also do away with a great deal of the social ostracism that accompanied the concept. Thereby taboo on the woman and members of the lower castes while performing or participating in any ritual or worship became inoperative.

Vijaya Ramaswamy, in her recent study on women, society and spirituality in South India *Walking Naked*, IIAS, 1997) has identified a list of 34 women saints among the Lingayats. She notes "the visible tension between the rejection of patriarchy at the physical worldly level by these women and their use of the patriarchal mode at the metaphysical level to express this very rejection of convention. For instance, Akka Mahadevi, perhaps the most well known woman among the *vacanakaras*, makes use of conventional notions of family in this vacana when she states

> I have Maya for mother-in-law, the world for father-in-law three brothers-in-law like tigers, and the husband's thoughts are full of laughing women no God, this man, and I cannot cross my sister-in-law.
>
> (Ramanujan, 1973, v 328)

Yet the depths of devotional fervour and the revolutionary content of their poetry as well as their spiritual aspirations cannot be contained with the merely conventional.

I would like to take up the poetry of Mahadeviakka as a case in point. Mahadevi was undoubtedly the most powerful and appealing of the Virasaiva women mystics. In her vacanas, she has expressed her devotional fervour in terms of *sati-pati-bhav*, or the feeling of the lord as husband and the bhakta as consort. Her vacanas point to the yearning for spiritual fulfillment through the attainment of *samarasya* or harmony between the *linga* and the *anga*. As in much of Bhakti poetry, her verse took on the form of the nayika-nayaka discourse, where she placed herself as the nayika waiting impatiently for her errant or wayward Divine Lover. The nayika-nayaka mode was one of the major poetic devices employed by the Bhakti poets regardless of gender, but in case of the women saints, the relationship, described is more intense, the discourse gynocentric and the physical overtones more real. In her poetry, Mahadeviakka makes use of very strong sexual imagery in her seeking for the ultimate union with the Divine. Here her imagery is startlingly bold and intense and there is no attempt to gloss over or cover up the sexual, but is blatantly direct in her descriptions of the body.

> In our embrace the bones should rattle in a welding, the welding mark even should disappear The knife should enter totally when the arrow enters, even the feathers should not be seen.
>
> (Chennaiah, 1974, 39)

Hagiographical accounts extol the extraordinary physical beauty of Mahadevi, popularly addressed as Akka meaning elder sister. They record that the king was so besotted by her beauty that he was intent on marrying her. But Mahadevi was so devoted to the idea of the union with her Divine lover that she could not even tolerate the suggestion of such temporal marital relations. Ironically enough, throughout her life, she was tortured by human beings who took interest in the beauty of her physical body. As a protest against being treated merely as an embodiment of sex, it is said that she discarded her garments and walked out of the palace naked. Later, as a concession to the people around her, she chose to wear her hair as a cover over herself. Evidences of this story are apparent from the texts of her vacanas. But she refused to accept wide spread notions of gender and the societally acceptable notion of the woman as the other, the temptress. Evidences of these ideas are manifest in her vacanas. For instance in one vacana, she states

> To a male ascetic, Maya takes the shape of a female ascetic: to a man she is a nun, a man to a woman, a woman to a man O Chenna Mallikarjuna, I am not One to fear this Maya of thine.
>
> (Menezes and Angadi, 1973, v 143)

Such fierce rebellion would naturally have its earthly consequences. She was called up by her guru to explain her deliberately rebellious act of discarding her garments and walking naked. At the Anubhava Mantapa where all the great ones gathered to listen to her defence, she justified her stance in public and also gained great respect in the tradition of *jangamma*, the ever moving. She was able to completely invert traditional ideas of gender in spirituality, when justifying her need for abandoning clothing. She retorts in an almost light-hearted vein, when she says

> To the shameless girl,
> Wearing Mallikarjuna's light, you fool,
> Where is the need for cover and jewel?
>
> (Ramanujan, 1973, v 129)

Yet the other members of the august gathering were able to discern the serious concerns of Mahadeviakka and quick to voice their encomiums. Prabhudeva records his perception of her spiritual journey in a vacana thus:

> Shedding her corporal traits,
> She has become united with the linga
> She has become
> Herself, the Supreme Light.
> I say hail to the majesty
> Of Mahadeviyakka, who has,
> Shedding the sense of self and other
> Become one with the Linga itself,
> In Guhesvara Linga.
> (Prabhudeva, *Sunvasampadane*, IV, XVI, 58)

Mahadeviakka was thereby able to completely subvert conventional notions of gender in her teachings as well as by precept. Her approach was truly revolutionary and even sensational, but could achieve the desired results.

Despite opposition from her own people and widespread social disapproval, she could, by her discourse through her vacanas as well as her actions, bring to the popular her own notions of gender which was singularly deviant from the conventions of her own time. The tensions that were created by such subversions are evidenced in the poetic language of her vacanas. In the explicitly sexual terms in which she describes her relation with her spiritual lover, she is unique and has been able to achieve a reordering of prevailing definitions of gender. Through both her words and her actions, she not only succeeded in voicing herself and giving due emphasis to her ideas but even rewrote gendered spirituality and created a new concept of gender for public notice. It is herein that we become aware of the revolutionary nature of her life and work.

Feminists of all variant attitudes, have with one voice fore-grounded the need for the private to be brought to public knowledge with regard to women's issues. In their very act of speaking out in a culture that silenced and marginalized the woman's voice, the woman mystics were revolutionary in their outlook. Through their discourse, where they interpreted and codified their personal experiences, in spiritual terms, they were able to find recourse to a unique mode of expression. Bhakti, with its adoption of a personalized tone and stylization of emotion in terms of the nayika-nayaka dialogues, gave these mystics an ideal situation to exploit their need for discourse. By its very nature of relating to the Divine, on an experiential plane, this form of devotion broke new grounds irrespective of class/creed and achieved much widespread acclaim. The position of the bhakta on a passive and submissive level in contradiction to the Spiritual, which was placed in a position of power, thereby replicating the woman's position in the socio-cultural strata, made this mode ideally suitable for women to express themselves. And by exploiting the situation to its very limits and making public, their spiritual, their private emotions and desires, these women did take up the "feminist" deals. But the language of their poetry and their social behaviour were often contradictory to each other thereby creating a spiritual dialectic. The dynamic tensions between their language and action, was, to a great extent, responsible for the native force of their poetic discourse. In the poetics of *bhakti* the woman's domestic role was in a sense accentuated and publicized in the socio-religious context creating a whole new mode of expression from the woman's point of view. By making use of oral discourse rather than the written, they subverted even the need for literacy in either the speaker or the listener. And within the given parameters, she was freed from mundane domesticities and even venerated on account of her public position.

But the true revolutionary content of their discourse has not yet been fully underscored. It is only when the women mystics are seen in the context of their socio-cultural ethos that the picture becomes clear. It is true that the Virasaiva ethos allowed much scope for gender sensitivity and freedom from the mundane. Poetic devices like the nayika-nayaka mode employed by all, irrespective of sex, nevertheless created a special niche for the woman mystic. Though the men assume the passive female role, the *lila* (play) is nevertheless seen and expressed from the phallocentric perspective, unlike the women whose voices ring more authentic in their representation of the yearning for their Lord.

Both the women mystics examined here, were venerated even during their time. Perhaps that is one of the reasons why their utterances are heard even today and preserved for posterity as a record of their having existed and having spoken out. Yet their discourses reveal the pain and intensity of disgrace they encountered. Feelings of shame and distaste over unwarranted male overtures are recorded by both the speakers analysed in this paper. Andal's conservative brahminical social attitude would perhaps have called for greater determination to break away from accepted conventions of her time and a much more acute sense of rebellion in the protagonist as recorded in the internal evidence of her poems. And the use of the oral medium perhaps accounts for the popularization and the dissemination of their work. But is it popular fear of their influence on the ordinary woman that has resulted in the idolization of these mystics? Both Andal and Mahadeviakka are today worshipped at temples and represented as avatars of the goddess. The recent film *Scribbles on Akka*, for instance, examines the transformation of this rebellious mystic into an icon of popular worship. Is the representing of the rebellious as divine a clever device of channelising feminine rebellion. By representing the unacceptable as divine, are they in a sense mainstreaming the legend and avoiding the revolutionary influence of their discourse which was both popular and eclectic? Is the idolization another phallocentric device of marginalizing'?

References

Dehejia, Vidya. *Antal and her Path of Love: Poems of a Woman Saint from South India* Albany: State University of New York Press, 1990.

French, Marlyn. "Is there a Feminist Aesthetics?" in *Aesthetics in Feminist Perspectives*. Ed. Hilda Hein and Carolyn Korsmeyer. Bloomington, Indiana, 1993. pp. 153-65.

Gadon, Elinor. *The Once and Future Goddess: A Symbol of Our Time.* New York, Harper and Collins, 1989.

Hardy, Friedhelm. *The Religious Culture of India: Power, Love and Wisdom*. Cambridge University Press, 1995.

Hudson, Dennis. "Bathing in Krishna: A Study in Vaishnava Hindu Theology" *Harvard Theological Review*, 73, 1980.

Kleinberg, Jay. *Retrieving Women's History: Changing Perceptions of the Role of Women in Politics and History* Paris: UNESCO Press, 1988.

Ramaswamy, Vijaya. *Walking Naked: Women, Society and Spirituality in* South India, Shimla, HAS, 1997.

Speaking of Siva. Translated and with an introduction by A.K. Ramanujan New York: Penguin, 1973.

Tharu, Susie and K. Lalitha. *Women Writings in India*, 1993.

The Azhwars: For the Love of God (Selections from the Nalayira Divya Prabandham) translated and with an introduction by P.S. Sundaram. New Delhi: Penguin, 1996.

7

"Modern" Indian Poetry in English: Some Critical Issues

Guillermo Rodriguez Martin

Any examination of the key issues and controversies that have been plaguing the critical agenda of so-called "Modern" Indian Poetry in English (I.P.E.) since the 1950s needs to attend to the historical development of I.P.E. and the critical appreciation of that particular body of poetry, starting from the first anthologies and works of criticism till the present. Most critical writing on I.P.E., especially (but not only) in the first decades after Independence, was produced by Indian critics who were poets themselves (belonging either to the new or "modernist" poets or to other, earlier schools), and thus a study of the critical scene of Modern I.P.E. should be closely connected to the poetics and critical practices developed by these poet-critics throughout the years. Another group of prominent critics writing on Modern I.P.E. is made up of western critics who became interested in what was initially termed Commonwealth Literature or New Literatures in English. A general pattern of critical practice and canon-making, which underlies the dynamics of I.P.E. criticism, comes to the surface only when a particular poetics encounters another and when its tenets are interrogated by a new generation of poets and commentators.

The moot points investigated here touch on the problematic of literary historiography in I.P.E., literary/cultural categories and aesthetic value systems. Western concepts like modern, modernism and modernity, which are commonly applied to post-Independence I.P.E., have a very wide semantic field as literary (aesthetic), historical (chronological), cultural and philosophical meanings converge in them. The problem is aggravated when these categories are adopted by Indian literary critics and poets to operate in a multi-cultural and multi-lingual environment. The following paper is a metacritical assessment of some of the critical issues related to historical and aesthetic concepts and concept-making in post-independence Indian Poetry in English.

Historical Analysis in I.P.E. Criticism

When analysing a particular poet's work or a poetic movement like modernism in post-Independence I.P.E, critics often lose sight of the historical development of Indian poetry written in English and in other Indian languages. Despite the fact that Indian poets have been writing in English for over 150 years, an in-depth analysis of its "slow evolution"[1] or something like a comprehensive "History" of Indian Poetry in English is yet to be produced.[2] Barring a few exceptions, most of the post-Independence poets and critics seem to be unwilling to acknowledge the historical dimension of poets, poems and poetics or "movements". Several reasons may be cited to explain this.

The very idea of a history of I.P.E., and with it the related concepts of a literary past, heritage or tradition, have been heavily debated. For instance, an eclectic critic like John Oliver Perry has for various reasons rejected the idea of a historical development in I.P.E., dispatching it either as a western conceptual construct or as a revivalist "ideological campaign". In a similar vein, A.K. Mehrotra and other post-independence poets have eschewed the past as something better to be forgotten, or have argued that I.P.E. is a tradition in "the making".[3]

The marginality issue also plays a role in this context. The English language and Indian poets writing in that language belonged for a long time mainly to the urban elite (academics and other middle-class professionals). Today, there are poets from all corners of India publishing in English, and it is not a culturally homogenous group. Yet, some commentators, like the poet K.N. Daruwalla and the American critic Bruce King, to name just two examples, have preferred to de-link post-Independence I.P.E. from the Indian regional cultures and thus from a local tradition, instead of placing it within a wider cross-cultural and cross-linguistic map. Against this attitude, a comparatist approach with regional language poetries is posited by comparativist scholars like Ayyappa Paniker and Vinay Dharwadker, and nativist-oriented critics like Makarand Paranjape, as being essential for a proper understanding of the history of I.P.E.: "*the only true history of Indian English poetry can be written only after that study* [of the varied interplay of Indian Poetry in English with that of the regional languages] has been completed".[4]

It is only in the late 1980s and 1990s, when a new generation of poets and critics born after Independence came to the fore which had not lived through the post-independence cultural crisis or struggle for self-definition, that an "inclusive" historical or historicist[5] perspective was brought into I.P.E. studies. It may be argued that it is historical distance, or the ability to look back from a distant vantage point, what allows for a more comfortable and comprehensive assessment of that which is already past or "miide."

The Validity of Western Terms: "Modernism" and "Modern"

The usefulness of these concepts in I.P.E. criticism and Indian literary criticism in general has often been questioned. Perry strongly criticises Bruce King in his landmark work, Absent Authority (1992) for employing western historical categories like modern and postmodern, which imply a viewpoint that "crassly [universalises] the Euro-centric historical "development" and value system." Perry's argument is that, since I.P.E. and its criticism lacks a "firmly operative tradition" and is thus essentially "non-historical" it shall better be described as being in the process of producing a "contemporary tradition."[6]

Since Perry is preoccupied with the shaping of a "contemporary" indigenous criticism for Indian literature in his critical work, he suggests that it should not be developed from a misleading western historiography:

> ...Indian English literature [is] essentially "contemporary, " not necessarily "modern" nor, though composed after 1947, properly "post-modern." Both those latter terms, no doubt, have some usefulness within Indian criticism for tracing the relevance of well-defined Western literary movements to Indian ones. Yet obviously not all Indian literature that is contemporary, or post-Independence, should be described and analysed according to those western dominated critical terms that emphasise the avant-garde.[7]

Nativist-inclined Indian critics agree that Indian literature and its criticism (including writing in English) should be operating in a non-western terminology. In his award-winning After Amnesia (1992), for example, G.N. Devy analyses crucial western concepts and assumptions inherited from the colonial experience:

> The key terms that appear in any account of modern Indian criticism are "colonialism," "Renaissance," "modernity" and "Westernization." The logic behind these terms is that colonialism triggered off the Indian Renaissance, and the impact of Westernization on literature was to endow it with modernity. It is assumed that the colonial impact caused the Indian attempt at a grand synthesis of the East and West, now termed "Renaissance," and that the assimilation of Western literary forms and critical paradigms led to the assertion of self-identity and modern self awareness in Indian literature.[8]

Devy himself uses the term "modern" in a variety of contexts in his work After Amnesia, which includes chapters on "Modern Indian Intellectuals and Western Thought," "Modern India and the Sanskrit Tradition," "Bhasa Literatures and the Modern Attitude" etc. In his latest essay of literary criticism "Of Many Heroes," An Indian Essay in Literary Historiography, published in 1998, he refrains from employing such western terminology gratuitously.

Whereas other academic critics of I.P.E. (besides Perry), like H.H. Annaiah Gowda,[9] S. Peeradina, Chirantana Kulshrestha,

Kaiser Haq, and P.K.J. Kurup have tried to avoid the term "modern" by replacing it with "contemporary," most anthologists from P. Lai's and Raghavendra Rao's 1959 anthology Modern Indo-Anglian Poetry to Mehrotra's Twelve Modern Indian Poets have preferred to use "modern" to refer to poetry after the 1950s.

Some confusion however, arises out of the fact that the terms "modern" and "modernist" were initially (in the fifties and sixties) adopted in I.P.E. criticism to define a specific poetics or a group of poets belonging to a poetic "movement" that was influenced by the European modernists and needed to be distinguished from the Romantic pre-Independence poets. In later years, "modern" came to be used also as a historical term to name a literary period in I.P.E., i.e., usually the poetry written after Independence, or after the 1960s, according to others.[10] The Multiple meanings of the terms "modern" and "modernism" in Western history and literary criticism, and the fact that, concerning Indian poetry, they can have Western and/or Indian connotations, make a precise reading of these categories in I.P.E. criticism more than difficult. In addition, Indian critics rarely qualify these terms when they make use of them.

A U.S. based critic like Vinay Dharwadker, for instance, understands as "modern Indian poetry", all the literary forms which appeared in India during the twentieth century, i.e. "the variety of movements, schools, factions, and styles that have shaped [modern Indian poetry in the major Indian languages including English] in the last hundred years or so." At the same time, Dharwadker makes also indirect use of the designation "modernism" to describe "a nation-wide movement that started in the 1930's [and] was the Indian counterpart of Anglo-American modernism."[11] Following Perry's suggestions, one could argue that, whereas the usefulness of the former historical term ("modern" understood as "modernity") is questionable in the Indian context, the latter application of modernism can be meaningful in that it traces "the relevance of [a] well-defined Western literary movement to [an] Indian one."[12]

Modernism as a Literary Import or as an Indigenous Historical Phenomenon

Critics generally refer to Indian poets writing in English in the fifties and sixties either as the "new" or the "modern/ist" poets. The western terms modern and modernist/modernism were adopted by Indian critics from Western literary history and applied to this new trend or movement in I.P.E. for mainly two reasons. Firstly, for lack of another English term as an alternative, besides the adjective "new," which was already in use in many regional languages to denote the changing trends that had surfaced in other Indian-language literatures. Secondly, since many of the "new" poets were said to have turned to British and American so-called early or high modernist poets as a source of inspiration. The western poets of the early twentieth century (Pound, Eliot, Auden etc.) had been widely read and studied by Indian poets writing in English. Moreover, many of the "new" Indian poets were English Literature teachers and academics. Indian poets had found that western modernist aesthetics, partly born out of the deep social changes of the inter-war period in Europe, had a relevance to their own context. And so, western modernist poetics provided a model to simply imitate or, in the best of cases, to absorb and indigenise creatively.

Most scholars and commentators of I.P.E. have maintained that a deep identity crisis (described sometimes as a typical post-colonial situation) drove them in search of new ways of expression and of aesthetic values that would address the needs of the individual as opposed to those of a nation. They differ, however, when assessing the extent to which this was a reflection of the profound social and political changes that had taken place in the post-Independence years in India. Moreover, when critics refer to the Indian social (urban or regional) context, they may do so with entirely different intentions: in some cases for comparative historical reasons (Dharwadker) or to assert the "authenticity" of modernist poetry (Parthasarathy), and thus its "Indianness", but also (interestingly) to justify the use of western terminology (King).

Regarding the impact of western literary movements like modernism, avant-garde, existentialism etc. on Indian poets, Dharwadker remarks:

> Using a range of [Western sources]...[Indian poets] concentrated on such themes as the disintegration of traditional communities and familiar cultural institutions, the alienation of the individual in urban society, the dissociation of thought and feeling, the disasters of modernisation, the ironies of daify existence, and the anguish of unresolved doubts and anxieties.[13]

Going by these observations, G.S. Frazer's description of modernism in the West as "an imaginative awareness of the stress of social change" could fit the Indian context quite well.[14]

Each regional version of modernism obviously had its own contexts, peculiarities and life-spans, but the new trends which emerged in Indian literature in the 1930s and 1940s and flourished in the fifties cannot, according to Dharwadker and other comparatist critics, be separated from the social changes (disintegration of traditional social structures etc.) that took place in India during that period. Modernist poetics and ideas from the West were able to "invade" India when the appropriate historical conditions for it had taken place, particularly among the urban classes: social change, disillusionment, identity crisis etc. The modernist stance was then to a certain extent "indigenised" which resulted in a new poetics for I.P.E. Or, in other words, when the need was there for a "modernist" expression, outside models were imported to suit the Indian context(s).

Bruce King, on the other side, only sporadically refers to the Indian social-historical context, and fits it into a Western idea of progress and development: "The new poetry was part of the post-independence modernisation of Indian society and emerged first in and is still often a phenomenon of the larger urban areas."[15] King has no use for a sociological criticism that looks at the particular Indian context(s).[16] As in other countries of the Commonwealth the "modernization" of Indian society brought forth a "modernization" of Indian writing in English, and "the better writers have moved from modernism to post-modernism" according to King. "It is clearly impossible" he feels, "to have the fruits of the modern and keep traditional culture."[17]

For entirely different reasons Indian poets, critics and anthologists in the 1960's and 50's struggled to proclaim the "Indianness" of Modern I.P.E. The abstract concept of Indianness was eventually rendered useless as a literary criterion, but served poets writing in English to assert their national identity and come out of a "freak situation".[18] The "new" poet and anthologist R. Parthasarathy needed to emphasise in several occasions that, despite its linguistic and cultural problematic, post-Independence (modern) Indian poetry written in English is rooted in its Indian environment and is an integral part of its culture and society.[19] To prove his point, he quoted a famous statement by Nissim Ezekiel, who is often called the pioneer of modern I.P.E: "India is simply my environment. A man can do something for and in his environment by being fully what he is, by not withdrawing from it. I have not withdrawn from India."[20] In the 1990's a few Indian critics, influenced by post-colonial theories and by a new trend of nativist critical writing, pointed out that Parthasarathy's widely read anthology Ten Twentieth Century Indian Poets (1976) was part of a paradoxical yet highly influential effort to claim the entire "Indian" nation-culture for a handful of poets writing poetry in English that fitted into the canon of an imported modernist poetics, which Parthasarathy himself followed.[21]

A more balanced double-fold approach to modernism in Indian poetry in English is recommended by the renowned post-independence academic critic and (less well known) poet Syed Amanuddin:

> There are two ways of looking at modernism in Indo-Anglian poetry, one as an Indian response to the spirit of modernism in British and American literature, and two, as a product of the stress of social and political changes in Indian life; Indo-Anglian poetry like the poetry of other former British dominions and colonies has both imported and indigenous elements.[22]

Likewise, the literary historian M.K. Naik has stated that alienation, the archetypal mode of the modern writer, has to be analysed in I.P.E. in the light of both the Western inputs and the "specific Indian context."[23] Refuting O.P. Bhatnagar's charges that alienation in the Indian poet in English was mainly an "elitist mode" and "the most easily borrowed fad."[24] Naik identifies "three broad aspects of the phenomenon of alienation" in the Indian English poet:

(i) alienation from the traditional religious ethos as an urban middle-class citizen,

(ii) alienation from accepted social-cultural mores; the poet is deeply affected by the contrast between the pre-Independence values and those of the modern age in India,

(iii) existential alienation.

He argues that "the theory and practice of western modernism naturally has a great attraction for [the Indian poet writing in English] and the resulting spirit of emulation may have intensified his alienation further.,"[25]

The interpretations given so far differ substantially from what G.N. Devy and Makarand Paranjape have to say on the arrival of modernism in India. Indian critics with a nativist agenda have their own reasons to describe modernism in India not as something that arose (even partly) out of an indigenous social, political or economic situation, but as an attitude that entered India through literary channels alone. Thus we have Devy's comparison of modernism in Europe and in India: "Modernism, which in Europe was a product of a genuine social upheaval and cultural breakdown, reached India through literary models rather than economic developments and social crisis."[26] Paranjape endorses a similar theory, which was already postulated by the scholar Mokashi-Punekar in 1978:

> Mokashi-Punekar surmises and rightly, I think, that the modernist sensibility in India owes itself chiefly to the influence of Eliot, Pound, Leavis, and Richards. In other words, its sources are literary rather than social or

> political; moreover they are imported and extraneous, rather than indigenous and locally engendered.[27]

Like Mokashi-Punekar and O.P. Bhatnagar before him, Paranjape assumes that "modernism to Indians was not so much "a fact of life" as an attitude" or "pose" that they learned [from the West].[28]

Modernism in I.P.E. as a Rejection of a "Useless" Tradition

There is in I.P.E. criticism almost a standard critical version of the literary-historical circumstances that affected Indian poetry written in English during a particular period when Nissim Ezekiel, P. Lai, Dom Moraes, A.K. Ramanujan and a number of other young poets appeared on the literary scene in 1950s and 1960s. The common belief that a modern Indian poetics and aesthetics in English developed out of this group of poets was fostered over the years by the modernist poets themselves through their anthologies and critical commentaries. Bruce King has given a detailed account of this version of I.P.E. literary history in his groundbreaking work Modern Indian Poetry in English (1987).[29] In the fifties and sixties, a relatively small group of poets, mainly concentrated in the big urban cities of Mumbai and Kolkota and with living experience in the West, are said to have radically changed the literary panorama of I.P.E. by reacting strongly against the romanticism, nationalism and mysticism of the earlier pre-Independence poets Sarojini Naidu, Aurobindo Ghose and Rabindranath Tagore.[30] Many of these new poets were reputedly influenced by the British and American modernists of the beginning of the century:

> In the fifties arose a school of poets who tried to turn their backs on the romantic tradition and write a verse more in tune with the age, its general temper and its literary ethos. They tried, with varying degrees of success, to naturalise in the Indian soil the modernistic elements derived from the poetic revolution effected by T.S. Eliot and others in the twentieth century British and American poetry?[31]

In valuing the new and avant-garde, these writers held a modernist poetics to be superior to the earlier grandiloquent poetic inclinations prevalent in India. It was by establishing the anthological form in I.P.E. that they were able to propagate their own "new" poetics and forge a canon which was tailored to their tastes as Indian professors of English practising not only a new type of poetry, but also American "New Criticism", which was the dominant mode of literary analysis in most Indian universities at that time. This is a key issue that affects not only I.P.E. but also the critical history of Modern I.P.E. It is said that the poetics of the early modernist or "new" Indian poets and poet-critics writing in English (Nissim Ezekiel, P. Lai and the Kavita manifesto, and later also Parthasarathy and Mehrotra) bear the indelible mark of T.S. Eliot. It is fairly easy to relate common practises in I.P.E. criticism, both by Western and Indian academic scholars, to the critical tenets of New Criticism which derived partly from T.S. Eliot and I.A. Richards's essays, and which were the reigning mode of critical thinking among writers and literary critics in India and the West for many decades. In the critical process of valuing or disregarding "tradition(s)" in I.P.E., Eliot's notion of a "usable past" may have been a very influential tool for Indian poets and critics.

The Present Condition: Modernism or Postmodernism

Since many critics and anthologists apply the term "modern" even to poetry written in the 1980s and 1990s, it could be argued that "postmodernist" or "post-modernist" features are not (yet) dominant in I.P.E., or that Indian Writing in English is indeed intrinsically "non-historical" or "non-modern", as Perry and Nandy have posited."[32] It could also be contended that contemporary Indian literary critics, and I.P.E. criticism in particular, are now in the process of identifying and constructing an indigenous historiography, honing a non-western theoretical framework out of their nativist or post-colonial agenda. A "postmodern" awareness is nonetheless fairly strong in criticism of Indian Fiction in English. "Postmodern" techniques are said to have been employed in many novels since the 1980s and in recent years "postmodernism" in Indian Fiction has been discussed in a number of critical works.[33]

Only a few of the established critics have openly acknowledged that a younger group of Indian poets writing in English have been taking new directions since the late eighties and nineties. A second "new" generation of poets and critics were able to find a space in the I.P.E. scene partly due to the interest shown in the early nineties by new commercial publishers of I.P.E. Indeed, in the early nineties a new phase in I.P.E. and criticism was being heralded by attention-hungry poets and critics. As with the anthologists in the 1960s, it was again a young "rebelling poet-critic", Makarand Paranjape, who took the reins of his generation by championing the post-modernist cause in two anthologies published in 1993: Indian English Poetry, a survey of poets from the initial stages in the 1820's until 1980, and An Anthology of New Indian English Poetry, which introduced a new group of poets born after 1950. These two anthologies approach post-Independence I.P.E. from a historical perspective and set the tone for a "postmodernist" discussion in I.P.E., as well as for new controversies:

> ...it is possible to argue that modernism in Indian poetry in English was a glibly and unconvincingly internalised Western imitation; that in its excesses it was insulting and destructive of Indian cultural traditions; that the modernists themselves have realised this and are going back to translation, bilingualism, and religious poetry....[34]

Paranjape firmly criticises Mehrotra's anthology Twelve Modern Indian Poets, published only a couple of years earlier, as an attempt to perpetuate the "modernist" canon:

> Mehrotra extends the scope of "modern" by including the newer poets [Agha Shahid Ali, Vikram Seth, Manohar Shetty]... By equating modern with "good" and by avoiding the use of "modernist," Mehrotra ensures the continuing currency of modernism. Apart from this extension there is little new about this anthology. Rather

> it well illustrates the modernists obsession with closure, hyper-selectivity, and conformity.[35]

A similar critique could be extended to Bruce King's Modern Indian Poetry in English (1987 and 2001), where the new poets of the 80's and 90's are considered as "modern" poets, alongside with the first generation of post-independence poets. Makarand Paranjape, using a radically different and rather challenging approach in his anthology New Indian Poetry in English, claims to be the first[36] I.P.E. critic to proclaim that "modernism is dead:"

> Modernism in Indian English poetry, with its notions of a literary avant-garde, its emotional restraint and repression, its preference for irony and scepticism over all other attitudes to life, its self-conscious and precious craftsmanship, its belief in the image as the supreme poetic device, its aloofness and alienation from India, its secular dogmatism, its outright rejection of the past, and, above all, its arrogant narcissism and self-absorption is, thankfully, now passe.[37]

Other critics have strongly disagreed with Paranjape and insist that such a proclamation was nonsense (e.g. Bruce King) or that "it is difficult to demarcate the line between Modernism and Post-modernism in Indian English Poetry."[38] According to his own comments, Paranjape was also the first to announce "the birth of postmodernism." He described postmodernism in India as an affirmation of not conformity, but "difference" whether of language, region, nationality, politics, ethnicity, gender, or sexual preference." The poets, according to him, "are also more comfortable with themselves, less insecure culturally, and consequently more self-assured artistically."[39] Yet Paranjape is not willing to adopt the western terms "modern" and "post-modern" gratuitously, for he is well aware of the peculiarities of the Indian context. In his response to a questionnaire on the state of criticism in India, he stresses the nativist point, giving his version of a tripartite relation in India:

> Speaking of the problematic of modernism/ postmodernism, we in India have our own unique contribution to make to it. For us the debate is not so

> much between modernity and postmodernity as between tradition, modernity and postmodemity. There is so much in our society that is not yet modern. That is why I believe that India is a space which allows coexistence of contradictory ideas and phenomena unlike the West which lives through substitution and suppression of the other. An interface between tradition and postmodernism offers exciting theoretical and ideological possibilities which are unavailable to the West.[40]

Makarand Paranjape, on the other hand, suggests a periodisation of I.P.E. which "uses a combination of prevailing political and poetic ideologies" to label the literary-historical phases of Indian poetry in English:

- 1825-1900: Colonialism
- 1900-1950: Nationalism
- 1950-1980: Modernism
- 1980 and after: Postmodernism

Paranjape gives these time frames on the basis of several somewhat paradoxical assumptions that testify to his post-modern position:

(i) There are no "clearly demarcated phases nor a consensus over how to characterise them."

(ii) Modernism became only the "dominant tone" after 1950, and thus there were modernist precedents before 1950 and poets writing in the Romantic tone after 1950.

(iii) Modernism died in the 1980's and has given way to post-modernism or a new phase in I.P.E.[41]

Curiously, history repeats itself here. As a post-modern poet and anthologist, Paranjape is employing the same empowering medium and critical strategy that the first modernist poet-anthologists of the late 1950s (starting with P. Lai and Raghavendra Rao in 1959) and later poet-anthologists up to Mehrotra (1992) availed themselves to declare the pre-Independence Romantic poetry dead.

If we travel back to the fifties, we may remember that Lai and his fellow Calcutta poets had claimed in the Kavita Manifesto of 1959 "that the phase of Indo-Anglian romanticism ended with Sarojini Naidu." Another poet of the "modern" generation, A.K. Mehrotra, declared in his anthology: "much of the poetry [that the term 'Indo-Anglian'] describes, especially that written between 1825 and 1945, is truly dead."[42] Paranjape represents a generation of poets and critics who value pre-Independence poetry within its historical context, and seek a continuous tradition in I.P.E., while they criticise the post-Independence modernists for their dissociation from their immediate predecessors. Yet this is precisely what his post-modernist "manifesto" pursues: a break with the earlier (modernist) generation.

These inevitable contradictions notwithstanding, for the new generation of Indian critics, many of whom also happen to be poets, the "post-modern" is a bridge with the past; not an abstract past as might have been claimed by the Romantics or Nationalists of the Indian Renaissance, but one that leads to the discovery of local particulars. This generation of poet-critics believes that postmodernity in India is a "celebration of difference" (Paranjape), and thus there can only be a plural poetics for the post-modern (or postmodern) poets, which embraces the diversity and complexity of India's heritage. In this sense the Indian "post-modernist" poets and critics, unlike their western counterparts, might realise the task of "healing the wounds" that the so-called rupture with the (pre-Independence) past, brought about by the modernists, could have caused.[43] Yet this task may just be part of the natural process of interrogating one's own critical agenda by questioning that of the immediate fore-fathers, which makes for a another kind of "difference": not only literary or aesthetic, but indeed historical, not a celebration, but a (re-)affirmation.

Notes

1. K. Ayyappa Paniker, ed., *Modern Indian Poetry in English* (N. Delhi: Sahitya Akademi, 1991), 14.
2. G.J.V. Prasad's Continuities in Indian English Poetry (Delhi: Pencraft International, 1999) was perhaps one of the first critical studies of the

entire history of Indian Poetry in English. Other works that include a historical survey of some Indian poets writing in English are: A.K. Mehrotra, *An Illustrated History of Indian Literature in English*, Delhi: Permanent Black, 2003. M.K. Naik, *History of Indian English Literature* (N. Delhi, Sahitya Akademi, 1981). The first scholar to attempt a critical history of this literature was K.R.S. Iyengar. His first works *Indo-Anglian Literature* (1943) and *The Indian Contribution to English Literature* (1945) are basically historical accounts concerned with defining the nature and scope of a (still) colonial literature. Even his famed *Indian Writing in English* (1962, 2nd edition 1973) was not able to properly record the important modernist developments of the post-colonial era. Iyengar, K.R.S. *Indo-Anglian Literature* (Bombay: International Book House, 1943). *The Indian Contribution to English Literature* (Bombay: Karnataka Publishing House, 1945).

3. John Oliver Perry, *Absent Authority: Issues in Contemporary Indian English Criticism* (N. Delhi: Sterling, 1992). A.K. Mehrotra, ed., The *Oxford India Anthology of Twelve Modern Indian Poets* (N. Delhi: O.U.P., 1992). R. Parthasarathy, "Indian English Verse: The Making of a Tradition", *Alien Voice: Perspectives on Commonwealth Literature*. Ed. Avadesh K. Srivastava (Lucknow: Printhouse Publ., 1981) 40-52.
4. Paniker A. Vinay Dharwadker in his anthology proposes a comparative study of all major Indian-language poetries. Vinay Dharwadker, "Afterword: Modern Indian Poetry and its Contexts", The Oxford *Anthology of Modern Indian Poetry*. Eds. Vinay Dharwadker and A.K. Ramanujan. (N. Delhi: O.U.P. 1994).
5. See Perry, "In Pursuit of the Archaic," *Mapping Cultural Spaces. Postcolonial Indian Literature in English. Essays in Honour of Nissim* Ezekiel Eds. N.E. Bharucha and Vrinda Nabar. (N. Delhi: Vision Books, 1998) 155. This essay is a review of Makarand Paranjape's anthology *Indian Poetry in English* (Madras: Macmillan, 1993).
6. Perry, Absent Authority 49, 280.
7. Perry, Absent Authority 49.
8. G.N. Devy, *After Amnesia Tradition and Change in Indian Literary Criticism* (N. Delhi: Orient Longman, 1992) 102. See also Makarand Paranjape, "Preface", *Nativism. Essays in Criticism*. Ed. Makarand Paranjape. (N. Delhi: Sahitya Akademi, 1997).
9. H.H. Anniah Gowda, "Contemporary Creative Writers in English in India," *The Literary Half-Yearly* 10.1 (1969): 17-39, and Gowda, "The Use of Images in Contemporary Indian Verse in English," *World Literature Written in English*, 20 (Nov. 1971): 61-76.

10. See B.K. Das, "Post-1960 Indian Poetry in English and the Making of the Indian English Idiom," *Indian English Literature since Independence*. Ed. K. Ayyappa Paniker (N. Delhi: Indian Association for English Studies, 1991), 114-23.
11. Dharwadker, 186-87.
12. Perry, Absent Authority 49.
13. Dharwadker 189-90.
14. G.S. Frazer, *The Modern Writer and his World* (Baltimore: Penguin Books, 1970) n.p.
15. Bruce King, *Modern Indian Poetry in English* (London: O.U.P., 1987), 11-12.
16. See Perry, Absent Authority 280.
17. Bruce King, "What is Home?," *Debonair* (September 1988): 65, quoted. in Perry 280 (underlining mine).
18. See Nandy, "Introduction", *Indian Poetry in English Today*. Ed. Pritish Nandy (N. Delhi: Sterling, 1973), 6.
19. R. Parthasarathy, "Introduction", *Ten Twentieth Century Indian Poets, and Parthasarathy*, "Indian English Verse: The Making of a Tradition" 42.
20. Nissim Ezekiel, "Naipaul's India and Mine", *New Writing in India*. Ed. Adil Jussawalla (Harmondsworth: 1974) 88, quoted in Parthasarathy, Ten Twentieth Century Indian Poets 5.
21. See Suman Gupta, "Reinserting Nation-People in Anthologies of Indian English Poetry", *Journal of Commonwealth Literature* 31.2 (1996): 101-115. Also Rajeev Patke, "Canons and Canon-Making in Indian Poetry in English", *Kavya Bharati* 3 (1991): 13-37, and Patke, "Once More unto the Canon or Rebottling Indian Poetry in English", *Kavya Bharati,* 5 (1993): 13-28.
22. Syed Amanuddin,. "Modernism in Indian Poetry in English," *World Poetry in English*. Ed. Syed Amanuddin (N. Delhi: Sterling, 1981) 45.
23. Naik, "Alienation and the contemporary Indian English Poet," *Studies in Indian English Literature*. M.K. Naik (N. Delhi: Sterling, 1987) 76.
24. O.P. Bhatnagar, "Introduction," *Rising Columns: Some Indian Poets in English* (Amravati, 1981), 5.
25. Naik, "Alienation and the Contemporary Indian English Poet," 76-77.
26. Devy, After Amnesia, 116.

27. Shankar Mokashi-Punekar, Theoretical and Practical Studies in Indo-English Literature (Dharwad: Karnatak University, 1978). Paranjape, *Indian Poetry in English,* 22.
28. Paranjape, *Indian Poetry in English,* 23-24.
29. King, *Modern Indian Poetry in English,* 11-90.
30. These three "isms" go often hand in hand in Indian writers. The poet Aurobindo Ghose, for instance, turned from political activist to mystic poet to spiritual guru. Tagore, also a nationalist, romantic poet and guru, wrote most of his poetry originally in Bengali and then translated it into English.
31. Naik, *History of Indian English Literature,* 192.
32. Perry , Absent, Authority 49, and Pritish Nandy, *Indian Poetry in English Today*, 74.
33. An often cited example of a postmodern Indian novel in English is Shashi Tharoor's *The Great Indian Novel* (1989). For a critical survey of postmodernism in fiction see Viney Kirpal, *The Postmodern Indian English Novel: Interrogating the 1980s and 1990s* (N. Delhi: Allied Publishers, 1996).
34. Paranjape, *Indian Poetry in English,* 25.
35. Paranjape, *Indian Poetry in English,* xvii-xviii.
36. See Paranjape, "Modernism and its Discontents" Mapping Cultural Spaces. Postcolonial Indian Literature in English Essays in Honour of Nissim Ezekiel 51.
37. Paranjape, "Preface," *An Anthology of New Indian English Poetry* (N. Delhi: Rupa & Co., 1993).
38. See K.N. Daruwalla, rev. of An Anthology of New Indian English Poetry, *Sunday Times*, 20-26 June 1993. The quote is from B.K. Das, "A Modernist Poet or a Post-Modernist? A study of Nissim Ezekiel's Poetry", Mapping Cultural Spaces. Postcolonial Indian Literature in English Essays in Honour of Nissim Ezekiel, 129.
39. Paranjape, "Preface," *An Anthology of New Indian English Poetry.*
40. Paranjape, "Indian (English) Criticism" 75.
41. The quotes are from Paranjape, *Indian Poetry in English* 8, 7, 19. The summary of his critical tenets is mine.
42. P. Lai and Raghavendra Rao, eds., *Modern Indo-Anglian Poetry* (N. Delhi: Kavita, 1959), Mehrotra.
43. Paranjape, "Modernism and its Discontents", 55.

8

The Story of My Experiments with Writing Life: Problematizing the Feminine Pen?

B. Chandrika

> Literature, I teach my students in the Hudsonian style, holds a mirror up to life. But, I add in the Chandramati manner, that this mirror is often concave or convex. The reflection it gives the reader may not be quite truthful to the original. The question of authenticity in treating the facts of life in fiction is as old as the first fiction itself. But when life is treated as such by writers of fiction, life winds itself back on the writer. This is especially so if the writer is a woman. I am going to share with you some of the experiences I had as a practitioner of the genre.

I began my career of writing rather early in life—at the age of 12 and I started with something that any one can write—criticism. It is said that *naatakaantyam kavitvam* (the playwright ends as a poet); but in my case it was *niruupanaantyam katha* the critic ends as a fiction writer). From 12 to 22 years, it was non-stop writing of fiction for me. Some of the stories were critically acclaimed and I basked in a wonderful fan mail. But then there were problems waiting for me.

I was an unmarried girl—a saleable commodity. My family was worried that my sale-value in the marriage market would go down with each story I write about love and man-woman relationship. How can an unmarried girl write a story like "Malathinu Veliyil" (Outside the Borough)? It was a story published in *Mathrubhumi Weekly* (I 972) when I was an undergraduate student. The protagonist is a woman who goes out in the evening to the beach all alone. That itself was an unimaginable concept in these days—a girl on the beach alone in the twilight. Now literature and films are full of such girls-, but then—I am 50 years old now, whereas when I wrote the story, I was hardly 18. My heroine's attraction for the opposite sex, her plotting to win over her friend's fiance—all these were relishing topics for the critics, but far from being relished at home.

The troubles at home brewed stronger as I dared into yet wilder zones of female experiences. In the "respectable" families of Kerala, there was a practice of isolating girls for 5 to 7 days when they menstruated. There were even separate huts built for the purpose called *Anchaampura*. Things were not so bad at my place, but my friends used to come up with miserable stories of their being isolated for no fault of their own. The path, the "unclean" body and the isolation—they were irresistible themes for me and I came up with the story "Murukkumpoovukal" (The Scarlet Flowers of the Murukku Tree). The tree of Murukku has flowers of flashing scarlet—people would not even look at them for long for fear that they might get conjunctivitis. I took those flowers as a symbol for menstruation and wrote the story about two couples. One of the men is a coward, and, intimidated by his conventional mother, confines the wife to *Anchaampura*. The other man, his brother-in-law, whose wife is also sent there by the mother, sneaks in at night and takes his wife out, asking her, "Should we waste such a beautiful night?"

I was a postgraduate student in the Government Women's College when *Vanitha* published the story. It created such a furore, this time not only in my family, but in college too. A teacher of mine, a spinster who had crossed the forties, yelled at me openly in class—" Aren't you ashamed to write such dirty stuff after studying Keats and Emily Dickinson?" My mother asked 'in despair, "What are you upto?"

I was terribly humiliated for glorifying the female body thus, or, as Helene Cixous has said, "the body". Now, when a girl like Sithara writes about a gang-raped girl in her story "Agni" and mentions the sanitary napkin which the male hands of the rapist remove after a moment of hesitation, she is acclaimed as being the bold, genuine female spirit. Sithara was unmarried when she published the story, and she has not written about any harassment on account of writing "Agni". Times have changed so fast that Sithara is now hailed as the champion of the women's cause.

The straw that broke the camel's back came with the story of the twin sisters that I published in Malayalanadu. The relaxed morals of one of the twins was more than what society could put up with. "Does it ever strike these delightful creatures that their little fingers were made to be kissed, not to be inked?... Are there no stockings to darn, no purses to make, no braces to embroider? My idea of a perfect woman lies one who can write, but won't." The famous words of George Lewis! I decided to be the PERFECT WOMAN. It was silence for me—a silence that lasted 18 long years!

I returned to the scene in 1993 with the pen-name of Chandramati and was noticed again in the literary world that was now brimming over with writers. It seemed as if every one has suddenly become a writer. They were using, jargons like Modernism, Postmodernism, Srtucturalism and Deconstruction. 18 years ago they were fighting over terms like Existentialism and Alienation. Terms change, I noticed with interest, but people don't. M. Mukundan who had kindly defined modernity to young writers like I a decade ago, was now busy defining postmodernism to a baffled audience.

The stories I wrote first as Chandramati—like "Aryavartanam", "Devigramam and "Nilathil Poru"—were realistic but with a difference; some critics have categorized them under the label "New Realism" along with stories by some other writers too. As a teacher of critical theories in the postgraduate classes of my college, I too was familiar with all the jargons of Post-modernism. Armed with them I entered the field with my first Post Modern story—"The [Post-modern] Story of Jyoti Viswanath." At the outset of the story itself I pointed out that the adjective "Post-modern" is "intended as a signpost to critics, who, otherwise, would attach it only to writers of their choice." I hope it is evident that the story was intended to ridicule Postmodernism 'in Malayalam. Let me quote one more part from the beginning of the story to substantiate my point:

"The reader is given full freedom to read this story without any prior sanction from the author, at one sitting or piecemeal. The reader can stop reading now itself and decide not to read it at all. If by any chance you are continuing to read, please feel free to break the reading wherever you like. *Such exorbitant freedom will be given only by Milan Kundera or Italo Calvino or some of our writers who imitate them. You can even edit this story or re-write any of its paragraphs.*" The author's satirical intentions, I hope, are obvious.

Jyoti Viswanath turned me overnight into a recognized post-modern writer in Malayalam. Established writers and critics acknowledged my existence and the name of Chandramati started appearing in critical articles on Malayalam fiction. When I declared that the story was written to ridicule Postmodernism, the readers took the statement as a big Post-modern joke. I ignored them in the Postmodern way and continued to write as I liked.

What intrigued me was the fact that so many of the postmodern gimmicks imported from the West were already present in ancient Indian literature. While working (on deputation from the college) as Executive Editor of the Sahitya Akademi project on Medieval Indian Literature, I was really surprised to note the self-reflexivity of some of the narratives and the metalepsis employed in the narratology of certain works like Mahabharatha, Ramayana, Panchatantra, Vikramaditya Tales etc. Ved Vyasa and Valmiki appeared as characters in their works and actively interacted with the characters of the stories—like Federman in English or Kochubava in Malayalam in the 20th century! So what is the relevance of the term "originality"? Is originality only a recycled matter? It is a question that still intrigues me.

The literary scene, by the time of my re-entry, had become fragmented into several categories. One of them was women's writing, Lalithambika Antharjanam and Saraswathiyamma, two former writers of Malayalam, can be said to represent two parallel strands of women's short fiction in Malayalam. The women writers of today can be categorized as belonging to the one or the other, depending on the moderate or radical stances they adopt. The radical writers grouped themselves under the umbrella of *Pennezhuthu*, a rough transformation of *ecriture feminine*. I had to resist the mantle from descending on me. Women's writing is a good term, self-explanatory. But unfortunately, the term *Pennezhuthu* was not exactly sexual politics in Kerala, for here it had acquired a political colouring too. I am not an activist—certainly that is not my way-and I have had no political leaning whatsoever. I had always voted for the best woman, not looking at the party. I agree with Matthew Arnold that a writer should be above all sorts of political and religious biases, that he or she should have the virtue of disinterestedness. That is the main reason why I am against *Pennezhuthu*. The non-idealized pictures of women in some of my stories like "Saisavam" (Childhood) and "Daivam Swargathil" (God is in Heaven) have been bitterly attacked by "female feminists" as anti-women stories. But I have to present the convex, concave as well as the true pictures of life.

I have my own reasons for taking a strong stance against *Pennezhuthu*. Other than the political link that makes it unpalatable for the non-conformists, such a labeling marks out the mainstream for man and leaves only the margin for women. Also, under this umbrella term, third-rate women writers basking in the political patronage will come up as major writers, leaving the real meritorious ones to struggle for survival. Reservation for women may do good in politics, but not in the field of writing—that is my personal belief.

Writing for me, has been therapeutical too. It was one of the means by which recently survived the onset of a fatal disease. Again, that was a dull period in my creative life, for being under chemotherapy I was press-shy. I never published any thing I wrote. Or it would be better to say that I never wrote anything to publish. I kept a journal in which I faithfully recorded—sometimes in prose, sometimes in verse—all my physical pain, mental fears and trepidations, as well as my spiritual dilemma. All the love and kindness showered upon me, all the unkind words some of the visitors dropped—all found their way as poems, short sketches and entries. Once the crabs left my body for, good, I was able to put them to shape as a booklet—An Interval in the *Land of the Crabs*. This will shortly go to press. When *The Malayala Manorama* published it in their annual number, it elicited unprecedented response from my readers. The cancer patients thanked me for giving them a ray of hope; the others said, coming from the pen of a creative writer, it reads like fiction. Little do they know that it is my survival tactic.

Let me assert that I am a woman writer, conscious of the issues that women have to face in present society, and reacting to them through my fiction. The problems that I had to face at the initial stages of my writing are no longer there 'in full force, and I enjoy the sight of the young women writers enjoying their freedom. Since writing the body is no longer taboo, they unleash their pens, shocking the male world. Wanting to be different and distinct I have left it behind me. Now I have resorted to humour and satire as more effective weapons for my social reflexes.

To conclude, writing life in a society that is going haywire offers its own challenges. Narrow fundamentalist feelings have begun to control life in general now. If one of the bad and ugly characters in any story by any writer belongs to any religion she will be accused of being biased against that particular religion. One cannot produce characters out of thin air— one has to locate and place them somewhere and this has become a major problem for the present writer. I have fictionalized this dilemma of the writer in the story "Uttaraadhunika Katha Prathisandhi" ("The Crisis in Postmodern Story"). Perhaps fictionalizing dilemmas would be the best way to overcome them.

9

Theoretical Perspective of Subalternity: A Different Approach to Literature and Culture

Lalitha Lenin

Introduction

A logical discussion of subalternity of any kind needs to be based on its epistemological premises. Epistemology, with its traditional roots set in philosophy, upholds strong limitations in its entry into the multi-disciplinary domain of information science that remoulds the very character of human communication today. Though the dynamics of representation is influenced by fast changes encompassing the new means and methods of communication, we tend to believe that they have not much to do with the familiar semiotics and critical theory in the literature and the arts. Increasing application of information and communication technology (ICT) in the arts and literature is obvious but, there is hesitation to explore the avenues of information science to facilitate better interpretation of the post modern world and its shifting paradigms. A cursory glance over the critical theories corroborates this view and suggests for further theoretical perspectives fitting to the cultural contexts under transformation. This would probably help a better definition of the concept of subalternity and related issues in representation and reading in creative realms.

Literary Theories and Information Science

We have profusely used literary theories over the years to analyse, describe, interpret, compare, and evaluate the representational exposition in the arts and literature. Theories of modernism, structuralism, post-structuralism, deconstruction and postmodernism have heavily loaded our recent discourses with a theoretical mystique. The protagonists of these theories seem to have drawn interdisciplinary resources from philosophy, sociology, language, anthropology, history, politics, and psychology, but less from information science. Along the process, a fresh array of social themes and their aesthetic implications to our sensibilities and cultural dynamics has come to focus. Colonialism, post-colonialism, communism, marxism, communalism, spiritualism, environmentalism, nationalism, regionalism, internationalism, globalism and terrorism are some of them. The problem of subalternity becomes so evident in them that the springboard of literary criticism is electrified by the dialectics of class conflicts characterised by increasing diversity of interests in postmodernism. This is an essential feature of a world that is abundant in information and hence vibrant in its behaviour. It is manifested well in its literary products too.

Some theoreticians of postmodernism interpret it in socio-economic terms and hold the view that it signifies a decentralised phase of the development of the market place. To some, it is a cultural change most favourable for eclectic choices. It undermines the value-based sensibilities of modernism and marks the end of meta-narratives. There is an unfolding of pluralism where we feel short of an adequate 'objective' account of reality. The digital divisions in the new forms of representations add to the intensity of this experience. The freedom in individualist choices and the agony of the fragmented inevitable go hand in hand providing a dualistic experience. It is emancipative for the mind from the existing structural weight of knowledge, but gradually reveals the disharmony germinating from the power conflicts embedded in multiple hierarchies.

The linguistic explorations of Chomsky and Derrida, the epistemological analysis of power structures by Foucault and the psycho-analytical studies of Lacan have been heavily utilised in critical theory. Derrida's deconstruction strikes an extremely different note on the concepts of 'text' and 'reading'. Here, the creative writing and reading are both cultural activities. The strategy of deconstruction interrogates the oppositional structures of meaning and thereby questions the hierachically organised conceptual orders. This has found a pivotal place in critical theory today and bears implications to the study of subalternity.

Foucault's approach has closer links with information for its epistemological foundations. Chomsky's research is on the complementary function of language and the mind and he hints at the significance of microlevel biological and linguistic explanations for which the modern natural sciences are not yet willing, to reduce the mental to the physical. Lacan's psycho-analytic plane concentrates on the study of the unconscious as a linguistic structure and proceeds to explain the real, imaginative and symbolic representations. This is also an area marked by oppositional structures and hence the hegemonic forces and the question of subalternity. Feminism finds a more comfortable position within Lacanian thoughts.

All these theories pursue the dynamics of representations in diverse dimensions. All of them deal explicitly or implicitly with supra and/or infrastructures within the individual, the society, the larger universe and the media. Though the semiotic principles underlying different representational media vary, there is need for some logic of representation that cuts across the semiotic media. Since all representations are signs but not the other way round, logic of representation that involves the intentionality becomes essential. Probably, it indicates the relevance of applying a sound theory of information for possible explorations.

Information Science is a meta-discipline that emerged in the aftermath of the Second World War, consequent to the quantum leaps in science and technology information and publications. It holds a strong social and human dimension beyond that of information technology with which we have equated it. It is also centred on the representation and organization of information and plays a central role in the evolution of information society.

Information society is generally understood as an inevitable change of phase in the cultural history of humanity. There is a new form of power that immerses people in a virtual reality of images and simulations. When the real and the unreal cannot be made out, the public is easily manipulated through intentional representations created by unscrupulous power. Emergence of new cultural icons and practices are part of that. It is a postmodern society where information is the chief economic, social and cultural motor. Information thus assumes the status of a master resource with the potential to harness all other resources, cognitive as well as physical. Information society places excessive emphasis on the generation, processing, storage, dissemination, distribution, utilization and evaluation of information. Information, for convenience, is equated with knowledge and hence knowledge industries are assigned extreme importance in planning and developmental processes. Information technology has been instrumental to the evolution of information society, but information science has a wider social dimension with its theoretical basis. There is need for more holistic and deeper explorations in the study of representational dynamics in this context.

Information

Hundreds of definitions exist on 'information' with no consensus on the underlying concept. To the philosophers, it is a category and they provide the most abstract and comprehensive range of definitions. In psychology, it is a variable dealing with sensory perception, comprehension and other psychological processes. In communication theory, information is embedded in the message that is represented by signals, symbols, and signs. Language takes up the representational function while providing the structure and serving as the most powerful medium for communication.

In a narrower sense, information is considered in terms of signals and messages for decisions involving no cognitive processing. Communication engineering, mathematical physics and cybernetics have defined information in this view. In the Mathematical Theory of Communication 'information is that which adds to a representation', that 'logically justifies alteration of, or reinforcement of a representation'. In Information

Theory, it is considered negative entropy because information is ordered data and entropy is a measure of disorder. In the extreme mechanistic view, information does not have meaning to exist. Human beings are just epiphenomena without having a component role in its creation/generation.

The trends in defining information in the narrower sense have strong association with the developments in information and communication technology. Perhaps, the imaginative poetic mind of T.S. Eliot could sense the flutter of the postmodern information society earlier to Norbert Wiener's conception of cybernetics as expressed in his poem, 'Chorus from the rock' in 1947:

> Where is wisdom, we have lost in knowledge,
> Where is knowledge, we have lost in information?

Probably, it made a note on the possible technological developments that would ignore the substrate of the mind which provided the microspace for signalling patterns of myriad complexities involving various levels of integration (or disintegration?) leading to changing phases in culture. It took more than one decade again for J.C.R. Licklider to describe the man-computer symbiosis which envisaged cooperative interaction between human mind and electronic computer to perform beyond calculations and to enter into the formulative phases of thinking.

Classification and Communication

Communication is essentially understood as a process of making up one's own personality through perception and symbolization. In communication, classification is concerned not only with the cognitive processing of records but their contexts too. The motivation or intentionality of the text is linked to the wider social context of cultures or problem at hand. Here, information is defined in simpler terms as that which is communicated. Communication by itself is a sharing process. Foucault says, "it is necessary also to distinguish power relations from relationships of communication which transmit information by means of a language, a system of signs or any other symbolic medium...Power relations, relationships of communication and objective capacities should not therefore be confused".

Information being a kind of energy brings changes in the state of knowledge of the recipient. In short, information is shared knowledge. The study of the signs, signals and symbols and their ontological and relational structures has its relevance in information science. But the metaphorical language of literary and artistic communication cuts across complex dimensions that are strange to the transparent methods of science communication. However, the need for structure in articulation and the key role of classification is very basic to every form of human communication.

The concept of class and the process of classification have been applied in the history of human discourses in several ways. Information science attributes to classification a central position as a cognitive resource. It is a neural necessity for communication. Classification is an intellectual resource that enables man for choices and development of structures in articulation. Every artefact manifests as structures conceived by man as individuals and institutions.

Classification derives this ability from its right for definitions. A perfect definition, if there is one possible, leaves no statements in the effective projection of the major characteristics of the class. A definition for an entity cannot remain stable for long as its boundaries are determined by the experiences of the authority who defined it.

Even the most objective knowledge of the sciences is subject to this limitation, in spite of the availability of sharp methodological and technological tools for exploring the material structures. As the representation in the arts and literature tends to be mimetic rather than factual, the subjectivity is greater and so more intense, transitional, transcendental and poly-dimensional in character. It leaves infinite and infinitesimal openings for the widening spectrum of imaginative interpretations and meanings. This increases the scope for redefinitions and continues to enrich the critical theory in turn.

The definitions, on the other hand, are influenced by the interests of the authorities behind them. The characteristics of the class, once identified, selected and established by the author/

artist, introduce rigidity into the underlying structure and seek its affirmation and sustenance through consensus. Consensus is achieved through the appeal it carries to the senses and interests of others. Power structures have a greater role in this regard.

In this sense, classification can be interpreted as the basic inbuilt tool in the human system of neural communication that wields and moulds the cultural processes forming part of every creative work. In short, representational dynamics is inherently linked to the classificatory infrastructure of human mind and its neural communications process.

Power Hierarchies and Subalternity

Classification, placed at the heart of communication, determines the structures of the discourses in the form of hierarchies. Each structure is an order in itself. Classification determines the underlying authority in the text and art work. The term 'subaltern' denotes a status below in rank and it implies resistance to order. At the same time, subalternity is an inevitable characteristic of classified order (hierarchies). Thus, subalternity in general is not a question. It has relevance to the context of specific classes and the why and how of classification in historical and cultural contexts. The concept of 'class' in this respect needs a redefinition to suit the classificatory process of communicating information. It agrees with Derrida that reading is a cultural process through which we deconstruct the order and content of the text.

The withering of modernism in the new perspective can be viewed as the result of information overload and the consequent challenges in structuring holistic systems. As a natural course, the fragmentation of meta structures has taken place. The postmodern structure provided space for many subaltern classes like feminist and dalit groups. Instead of switching nostalgically back to modernism, new conglomerations of empowering subaltern cultures on a regional basis may prove more fruitful. But the challenges ahead are many when new configurations are attempted through contemporary writings. The foremost question to be answered is 'whose writings—the subaltern or upper class?' For those who consider this a question absurd, remains a further set of questions to be answered—"Can we revive the renaissance spirit of self-renewal for a fresh and healthy interaction for the coexistence and development of eclectic cultures? If so, how can we deconstruct the representational structures in the arts and literature in an expanding global information society which is committed to material development alone?"

References

Chomsky, Noam. New horizons in the study of language and mind. Cambridge: Cambridge University Press, 2000.

Debons, A. Information science: An integrated view. Boston: G.K.Hall & Co., 1988.

Derrida, Jacques. 'Of grammatology', tr. by Gayatri Chakravorty Spivak, Delhi: Motilal Banarasidas, 1994.

Eliot, T.S. 'Chorus from the rock'. London: Faber, 1947.

Foucault, Michel. 'Aesthetics, method, and epistemology', ed. by James D. Faubion, tr. by Robert Hurley and others. London: Penguin, 1994.

Foucault, Michel. The subject and power. In Foucault, Critical inquiry. Chicago: University of Chicago Press, 1982, pp. 777-795.

Foucault, Michel. Power/Knowledge: Selected interviews and other writings, 1972-1977, edited by Colin Gordon. Brighton: The Harvester Press, 1980.

Hannabuss, Stuart. 'Foucault's view of knowledge' Aslib Proceedings 48 (4) 1996: 87-102.

Lalitha Lenin. 'Politics of knowledge and woman'. Samyukata : *A Journal of Women's Studies* 1 (1) 2001:107-110.

Licklider, J.C.R. Man-computer symbiosis. (1960) reprinted in Paul A. Mayer, Computer media and communication: A reader. New York: Oxford University Press, 1999, pp. 58-71.

McGarry, Kevin. 'The changing context of information: An introductory analysis', 2nd ed. London: Library Association, 1993.

Ranganathan, S.R. 'Classification and communication'. Bangalore: Sarada Ranganathan Endowment for Library Science, 1951.

Ranganathan, S. R. 'Prolegomena to library classification', 3rd ed. Bangalore: Ranganathan Endowment for Library Science, 1967.

Saracevic, Tefko. 'Information science'. *Journal of the American Society for Information Science* 50(12) 1999: 1051-1063.

Shannon, Claude and Weaver, Warren. 'The Mathematical Theory of Communication'. Chicago: University of Illinois Press, 1949.

Sinha, Chris. Language and representation: A socio-naturalistic approach to human development. New York: New York University Press, 1988.

Wiener, Norbert. Cybernetics: control and communication in man and machine. Cambridge (Mass.): MIT Press, 1948.

10

Modernism, Post-modernism, Creativity and Colonialism in Malayalam Literature

M.G.S. Narayanan

It has become fashionable among critics to indulge in the fireworks of modernist and post-modernist Jargon, obviously in a bid to perplex tile poor reader. The modernist and the post-modernist in the West invented then new phraseology to convey something different from their existing tradition, some new experience related to social change in the twentieth century, following the two World Wars which shattered all values and banished all finer sentiments from life. They were the victims of then own enlightenment faith in progress, equality and peace. Then predicament was unenviable. This agony gave birth to cynicism about human nature and the future of civilization.

Bookish Indian scholars who never went through the hell and horror of such European war-experience, but blindly aped their counterparts in the West, cut sorry figures in their comic roles as critics. Tile pretentious and hollow preaching shows the distance between them and the realities of life among the people. The artist, the poet, the fiction writer has to be an organic part of life in the society in which lie lives and moves, breaths and thinks, and shared the passion of human existence. Living in an ivory tower, or pretending to live there, is an act of snobbery in a fools' paradise,—no, in a fools' inferno, if there is one. In Kerala, fortunately for us, we had a bunch of writers who were steeped in tile passions, witch moved the people—poverty, betrayal in love, inequality, dishonesty, perversion, ambition, disillusionment and frustration. Their work has been rooted in our tradition, its strength and its weaknesses. They did not need the modernist jargon to justify or legitimize their work. They stood firmly on our soil, but they could absorb the craft and the techniques of their Western contemporaries. Some of these were S.K. Pottekkaat, who wrote about simple country love (Naadan Premam), Takazhi Sivasankara Pillai who wrote the epic of his village in a big volume (Kayar), the great inimitable Basheer, the only Basheer, who picked up the destitute as his immortal characters (Aana Vaariyum Ponkurisum). In their own time, some critics had written openly, and others went on with a whispering campaign, to the effect that some of their stories were imitations of Mopasang, Chechov, Steinbek and others. Did they steel or imitate? 'Yes', in one sense, and 'no' in another sense. Kesari Balakrishna Pillai was the mentor and the guide for some of them. He had thrown open the gates of European literature. They all certainly read and enjoyed the best short stories and the best novels that came from the West. They must have felt inspired. They must have seen parallels between characters and life experiences in European literature on the one hand, and real life in India. There were certainly many similarities in the problems and patterns of life in modernizing societies. But they metamorphosed very thing they borrowed with the magic touch of then genius, with the result that their characters are typical Keralites from contemporary society. Their life situations were similar to what could have obtained in Kerala. From Chandu Menon's Indulekha to Changampuzha's Ramanan, all through the works of storytellers and poets, you can catch elusive glimpses of Western authors, philosophies, moments and styles. This is true of T. Padmanabhan, M.T. Vasudevan Nair, Vallathol, Asan, Sankara Kurup, Vailoppilli, Sugatha Kumari, Vishnu Narayanan Nambootiri, and Valsala, almost every contemporary writer who wrote well and got enthroned in the hearts of Keralites. Only a few like Ponkunnam Varkey and Kesava Dev among storywriters, and Kunhi Raman Nair, Edasseri and Akkitham among poets, have been almost total strangers to Western literature. However, they too were consciously or unconsciously, directly or indirectly, brought Western influence.

Some critics pointed out that Sankara Kurup imported mysticism and symbolism in Malayalam poetry. Others claimed that Edappalli Raghavan Pillai and Changampuzha Krishna Pillai imitated the romantic lyrics of Keats, Shelly etc. Takazhi, who created *Chemmeen,* had followed in the footsteps of Hemingway, the author of *Old Man and the Sea*. O.V Vijayan had reproduced the plot of a Maharashtrian writer, or was it a Hindi writer? The story of a single-teacher school, said other critics. M.T. had echoed a well-known Hindi writer in *Mist*, according to some one.

Well, these cases are not even worth investigation. Even if they are proved, they prove nothing, because in all these cases, it is not the foreign seed, or artificial manure, or the machine packing or the advertisement that has made the poem or story significant for Keralites. They have enjoyed it as their own, because it carries as its birthmark the flavour of the native soil, the genius of the Malayalam language. And when it comes to language, a language in the creative context is not merely a language, a man-made tool with prescribed grammar, but an organic being, a deity if volt like, who has her own love life that cannot be forced or purchased. No master or mistress of Malayalam language whose characters are remembered or lines are quoted or memorized, can be called a fake. I had occasion to move closely and intimately for many years with at least one of these master creators in contemporary Malayalam language P.C. Kuttykrishnan, who wrote with the pen name Uroob and wrote novels and short stories about the previous generation and the present generation. Though not "educated" in the formal sense, he had mastered enough English to understand some of the best fiction and poetry available in English language. He was very proud of that and even boastful. He was very outspoken in his comments about friends and enemies, politicians, prominent citizens etc. at least in the small circle of close friends. We spent several evenings going far into the midnight and shared books, thoughts and eatables. Though much elder to me in years, he treated me like an equal and put some faith in my ability to appreciate literature. From these experiences and from contacts with some other masters with whom I was not so close, I have known that whatever they borrowed from other countries and societies, they drew most upon their own childhood, home environment and early adolescence. This means that they possessed a reservoir of spiritual energy that enabled them to internalize much that they encountered. Whatever came later through reading or living, they pushed into a frame that was already formed in early life.

The genuine writer finds his first love in every other girl that he or she admires in later life. He or she reproduces unconsciously his/her own early situation in every human situation that he draws ill words, with umpteen permutations and combinations in details. His characters are drawn from the model characters in and around the parental family, school and city or village. He/she may enlarge them or distort them, but if you scratch their skin, you find his mother and father, sisters and brothers, teachers and rivals recreated from memory, which of course plays many tricks with reality. He cannot liberate himself from his subconscious mind in his creative moments. He may be describing all emperor or saint, but a shadow of his father or uncle or teacher must be lurking there. The battlefield in creative fiction is the camouflaged scene of a country courtyard where children have been fighting for ages. The love triangles are not far from his wishful thinking in the daydreams of adolescence. I mean they have to be so, if they happen to be impressive. Psychologists tell us that deep instincts, perhaps dictated by the genes and the DNA structure, determined our choices in company, career, working, reading, philosophy, rituals and hatreds or desires. These instincts are the instincts powerful when they are least understood, seeking outward expression through compulsive action like producing poems or stories. Only such creations are capable of making an impact on society and surviving beyond their own age.

When there is a temporary withdrawal from outside world—all the inner conflicts and sufferings and unfinished drama of life are carried inevitably by the self when such withdrawal occurs—the dream world and the daydream world take charge. Creative activity takes place in the twilight of consciousness.

It is the mysterious process that gives birth to art and literature. For this to happen, the artist or writer has to come out of all forms of hypocrisy and feigned passions based on experience in other societies that are totally strange to the members of the present society in India. Imitation and creativity are contrary to each other. Imitation may help the development of craft through repeated practice. However, the end of imitation marks the beginning of creativity; and the end of creativity marks the advent of self-imitation and pompous proclamations about the latest fashionable isms and slogans. When the spring of creativity starts drying up, or in a situation where it is not opened at all, jargons are employed to cover-up the deficiency.

In Kerala, such trends are noticed among a few critics, and often surface in periodicals, but on the whole, this cancerous growth has not affected the mainstream of literature and culture. The chief players in the fields of arts and literature, whether it is Sugatha Kumari, Akkitham, O.N.V. Kurup, Vishnu Narayanan Nambootiri or Balachandran or Vinayachandran or Vijaya Lakshmi—all these poets have been drinking deep from the perennial waters of our classical tradition and drawing tile strength to promote humanism and protest against the delays and distortions of Justice. The same is the case with our veteran storytellers like Vijayan or Padmanabhan, M.T. Vasirdevan Nair or Madhavikkutty, N.P. Moliainmed or U.A. Khader, Anand or Mukundan. They have then, feet planted firmly on social reality that represents unbroken continuity of culture with openness and tolerance.

Among poets, Ayyappa Panikkar, N.N. Kakkad, Arroor Ravi Varma and K.G. Sankara Pillai have been hailed at one time or other as Modernists. Some of them proudly acknowledged it also. Some of them wrote good poetry but some of their poetry is unimaginably dry and dull. Sometimes, Kakkad claimed to be a modernist and a follower of T.S. Eliot, the famous author of Wasteland, reflecting the post-World War mood of desperation, frustration and cynicism. However, it appears that Kakkad was closer to the neoclassicism of Eliot rather than his modernism. He was a good scholar and Sanskritist, and steeped in Vedic lore. He also used Sanskrit passages inserted into his Malayalam verses. It is this superficial feature, a matter of style rather than content, that made some half-backed scholars compare Kakkad with Elliot who was deeply into the Latin spirit. At one stage, Kakkad himself shook free of this dubious title. Though he was often difficult and obscure, on account of his Sanskrit bias, Kakkad has also written good romantic poetry as in Saphalamee yatra—recording a nostalgic view of his past love life and poetic efforts. Towards the end of his short life, he claimed that he did not like the attribution of modernity by some critics. Arroor is different from other poets in that he always shunned the smooth musical sounds and sentiments, but this is the only modernity about him. He is more in love with the permanent loyalties of life. His poetry is remembered for his biting epigrammatic remarks and firm stand against hypocrisy and humbug. Ayyappa Panikkar is more admired as a critic and a satirist though he perhaps likes his own role more as a poet. He is erudite and sensitive, and there is nothing of the frustration and anarchy of the European modernists in his life or poetry. K.G. Sankara Pillai is brilliant in his ideas, but critics who failed to understand him should have called him modernist because they confused modernity with obscurity—some of them have even called him post-modernist, because he seemed to be more inaccessible than others. If a simple love of experimentation with form and life is modernity, all of these are examples of modernity. If a natural predilection towards the extreme left, especially the revolutionary Communists or Naxalites who struck a sympathetic chord in the heart of every youth protesting against injustice can be termed modernism, all these poets can be accused of it in some measure. But that would be a strange definition of modernity indeed!—certainly a far cry from what is known by that name in Europe. What is common to all these poets is their sound scholarship in modern Western literature. In reading culture, they are typically modern, but in writing culture, each one is different, rebellious against tradition but ultimately in line with twentieth century democratic liberalism in modern India. However, modern India has nothing in common with modernity in European poetry. Our society is just entering the struggles and conflicts of early industrial society similar to what Europe experienced in the 19th and early 20th centuries.

An interesting new development in the field of critical writing in Malayalam language is the introduction of what is called postmodernism. This has been there for about two decades.

A group of writers, mostly teachers of philosophy, history and literature in colleges and universities, familiar with Western theoretical writing, have imported into Malayalam a large number of technical terms. They are the self-styled advocates of post-modernism. Their language is not the ordinary Malayalam known to native speakers, not even the artificial journalistic abracadabra, but a new artificial language full of obscure terminology. To what extent this is meant to clarify the meaning, and to what extent it is deliberately employed in place and out of place to befuddle and frighten the reader into surrender is not easy to decide.

It must be admitted that new terms have to be coined in a language if you have to express new concepts and experience. However, if life in one's own society does not produce them, and they are imported from another distant society about which you have only bookish knowledge, the chances of tolerance are bleak. They continue to remain foreign bodies without being assimilated.

These new terms were not creations but translations from English, though readers ignorant of this process often took them as the indication of original thinking and hailed the writers as new thinkers. The writers also encouraged this attitude through pretensions and proclamations of loyalty. What they were actually doing was to import European or American terms and debates, sometimes even without referring to their European pedigree. Some of the mutually contradictory concepts were jumbled and promoted at the same time indiscriminately in Kerala, and paraded as well as received as an extension of Marxism! The craze for things foreign, and especially the latest fashions in foreign (Western) countries, among the neo-literate sections of the people created a blooming market for such works. This behaviour on the part of writers and then-clientele may be taken as the typical expression of intellectual colonialism in the post-colonial era.

The strange thing about it is that such scholars even started identifying some identity, recent works in Malayalam, mostly short stories, as the product of post-modernism. In a society where even modernism, as understood in the West, is a concept of dubious relevance, the protagonists of post-modernism were making a bid to be recognized and leaned as the revolutionary prophets of a new movement. They were successful to a certain extent, being able to enlist support from teenagers in colleges, neo-literates and half-literates eagerly looking for sensationalism and adventure. These people welcomed as great new big ideas what they could not understand properly. In this period of the proliferation of printing techniques, many publishers came forward to exploit the trend for commercial advantage.

The result was all round concision among students of literature and culture, but this development need not be condemned as entirely negative. The over-enthusiasm and misplaced expectation produced a sober assessment of literary works at least in some circles. The debate that followed in the highly sensitive print media in Malayalam has already led to a reassessment of creative works, old and new.

Who were the real culprits, the critics or the creative writers, or both of them? It is interesting to note that many of the protagonists of post-modernism who glorified and celebrated *Ganja* and *Charas*, brutal violence and permissive sex life and championed complete anarchy Naxalite revolution, were meek and mild citizens in their private life, conservative in family relations and orthodox in religious and political attitudes. They might have indulged in sexual excesses and sown their oats at some stage status and income, but nothing more. These gentlemen-revolutionaries had succeeded in getting into safe and secure jobs, often high-paid jobs, for themselves, their children and relatives. They lived and moved in urban middle class society with complete ease. Not only that, they were not misfits or outsiders in society though some of them created such models in imitation of European novels in their literature.

For instance, Kakkanadan, the self-styled post-modernist, wrote a novel called Ushnamekhala on small pox, reproducing closely the atmosphere in Albert Camus' famous novel, the Plague. Futile sense of exasperation and uncertainty in society following the breaking out of the terrible epidemic of plague was responsible for the disintegration of the value system and the mad pursuit of momentary pleasures in sex in violation of all the social taboos. Similar scenes are described in Kakkanadan's novel also, though even an ordinary reader could see that such situations are not associated with smallpox in India. This type of novels and short stories had good sales, not probably on account of their so-called post-modernism, but in spite of it, for the vulgar sex vulgarly portrayed, with a clear eye on commercial gain ("Mankachi is better than tender coconut").

Mukundan of Mahe is another storyteller, for long resident in Delhi, and serving in the French embassy. He knows French and has successfully recreated many techniques of modern authors in French novels, exploiting them admirably to produce intimate accounts of Malayalee life in his native village. His craft is modern, fashioned upon the French works, but his characters and situations are his own, spontaneously arising out of the soil in the special environment of Mahe in Kerala. He has been for long in the front rank of creative writers in Malayalam language. However, he wrote a short story called 'Delhi' which reads like a horror story, quite out of tune with the rest of his output in literature. Immediately, he was hailed as a post-modernist, exposing the anarchical underworld inhabited by criminal gangs and millionaires. Probably, he wrote the piece with an experimental urge, and his fans took it too seriously. For his part, he did not repeat the performance and kept mum, neither accepting nor discarding the allegations of post-modernism.

N.S. Madhavan is another good writer, author of several powerful short stories, who has consciously donned the mantle of post-modernism. He selected strange and exotic themes and even stranger titles like *Higuita* for his stories, and made use of broken images, mystery and modern craft that have made readers put him in the category of post-modern writers. Again, he is just another brilliant bureaucrat in the Indian Administrative Service as far as life style is concerned, steadily climbing the ladder of promotion. This is not the picture that is found in the case of post-modernist writers in the West, critics or authors of creative fiction. They are the genuine martyrs of the crisis of civilization. Their aesthetic sensibilities made them revolt against the establishment, seek refuge in philosophy and live as outsiders in society. They broke the prescribed rules of conduct in respectable society and received the natural punishment through alienation, going mad or getting infected, often perishing in asylums or slums. For them, life was brutal, selfish or short. Their expressions of suffering, anxiety, frustration and protest were straightforward and genuine, and they paid the price for revolt with their own lives. On the other hand, our Malayalee pretenders have done nothing but pay lip service to post-modernism and make a name and profit for themselves.

Paul Zacharia is (or was?) another distinguished and famous short story writer who contributed a number of good stories in which he used modern themes and techniques with great competence. He also employed sex with great effect for venomous communal and political propaganda as illustrated by his erotic story about the Vivekananda rock and the Tehelka website story about a foreign student of Indian culture. Though some critics have called him post-modernist, he would better be considered as a modernist in the realm of short story. It is a pity that he has moved more and more into the field of sensational journalism, and has developed an obsession with fascism, abusing and branding every other writer, poet, fiction writer and essayist, with an intolerance unsurpassed in Malayalam literature. Sarah Joseph is out and out feminist with a vengeance, and post-modernist to the extent to which feminism forms an integral part of post-modernism. Now it is up to life in modern Kerala to catch up with post-modernism in literature!

11

British Intervention and Development of People's Information Systems in Kerala

R. Raman Nair

Society's need initiating its younger members into a definite state of knowledge seems to reach back into man's primitive states of evolution. It is this motive that led to the invention of writing which can communicate knowledge through space and time, and in the birth of the institution which is to store and disseminate the accumulated knowledge of society to its members.

The existence of and access to such social accumulation of knowledge is utmost significance the relationship it establishes between society and its single members. Society has to transient to the individual a required portion of knowledge in the interest of common welfare. Any member should also be able to draw at will the required knowledge from the store knowledge. Unless this accumulated knowledge is active in society, an individual will not be able to perform his due function as a member of society and contribute positively to the welfare of society. So the society will not be able to conduct its communal life on the highest level, which is actually possible.

Library Science is a social science and librarianship is ultimately social in its purpose. According to Måurice B. Line, librarianship is a communication between knowledge and society. All social systems are the result of unending evolution, which extends over centuries, which derives their factors from its different stages and systems, the common traditions and customs and laws and decrees passed by rulers in different ages to make the institution more useful to greatest possible numbers. So, library movement and library and information systems of a particular region can be fully a predestined and evaluated only through an understanding and analysis of the influences that reached it through time and space.

Ancient Indian Libraries

India has got a very ancient history of library systems, techniques and laws. Right from days of antiquity, Indian culture, philosophy and religion occupied a place of pride throughout the world and the neighbouring countries were all under the magic spell of its splendour and magnificence. Thousands of scholars from all over the world took hazardous journeys to use the huge collections of our recorded knowledge arranged in the most helpful sequence in our ancient seats of learning. These collections of documents were open to all irrespective of caste, creed or region for any length of time. Even free boarding, and lodging facilities were given to the needy users from far away places, for the period during which they used the collection. Even though were known as academic libraries; those at Nalanda, Taxila and Pataliputra showed freer public library character than any of the present day libraries of that size.

Education in Ancient Kerala

Kerala, the southern State of India also has got a library history parallel to that of India. The beginning of educational and cultural activity in Kerala may also be traced back to very ancient times. In ancient period, Kerala as an integral part of the socio-cultural unit called Tamilakam formed part of the educational system of Tamils. As in other parts of India in Tamilakam also, religion influenced all aspects of life, especially education. Theology laid down the law and the rule of conduct. Among them was the faith that free gift to knowledge and its carrier-books as charity would earn merit for the giver and that this merit could be exchanged beneficially in the life after death. For example, according to Manu the ancient codifier of law in India, free book service would earn even more of merit than the gift of the whole earth. Thus, religion was one generator of force leading to free book service in those ancient days.

Collections of recorded information formed an integral part of the education in Kerala from very ancient days. The places where collections of manuscripts were maintained were considered as important centers of learning and most significant place of education and wisdom. There is an ancient Sanskrit saying, which means that to have a library is to be an educator. This gives us an idea of the prestige, privilege and responsibility of one who possessed a library.

Many stanzas of the Sangam work *Purananuru* tells us that in those days common people were very much aware of the importance of education and collections of manuscripts. Stanza 3-12 of *Purananuru* a classic of Sangam period states that it is the duty of father to educate his son so that he will become virtuous. Education was also not considered a too formal process limited within any age group or other boundaries. Avvaiar, the most revered Sangam saint poetess advises to the young: "learn while young; letter and number, claim esteem; avoid ignorance, covet to be versed in knowledge, learn all sciences and cease not to learn." During those days, there were facilities to proceed studies on any division of knowledge informally by any one who has interest.

Scholar Home Public Libraries

The nature of the ancient libraries of Kerala was highly related to the education system of the people. The teaching- learning method followed in ancient Kerala was the same practiced in Gurukula System of education throughout India at that time. In ancient literature of South India, there are copious references to teachers who would arrange for the teaching and maintenance of boarding and lodging of students. The great scholars molded their family situations in a way in which it would blend with teaching-learning process, which they are to undertake. This resulted in hereditary specialization by families in specific subject fields. There were families in Kerala, which specialized in particular subjects like Thaikkatt Illam in Architecture. In Ayurveda, Indian system of medicine, there were eight great families, hereditary custodians of the science and practice of medicine well known throughout India. In martial arts, in astrology, even in literature we can find families maintaining such tradition. These houses can be compared to the subject departments of the present day universities or specialized research institutions. Access to them was freer than the present days. Qualification was purely merit and devotion. But inside, life and work was more strict and tough than we people can imagine in our present day situations.

It goes without saying that these scholar houses possessed great wealth of manuscripts on their topic of interest for the use of teachers, students and the interested users who came searching for them. Many original works and commentaries were written there. Each of the generations added their contribution to these collections. These collections of knowledge were undoubtedly neatly classified and catalogued and preserved in the best possible manner with reverence by persons who have familiarity with the thought content of these documents. Still Kerala maintains this tradition in some subject fields like martial arts, music, Ayurveda, dance etc. and at these ancient houses we can still see huge collections of valuable manuscripts on their subjects preserved with utmost care for use.

This was the library situation of ancient Kerala after manuscripts and other ancient forms of books became popular. They are to be considered as public libraries for their difference they had with the Institutions, which we call public libraries, was their specialization, which gives them an academic library character. But their services were available to all seekers and not limited to students. More than that, different collections of various subjects that existed formed together a network without itself being aware of it. In their totality they formed a system almost like our public library system. Specialization of units gave them efficiency.

Library Services by Government

The South was also familiar with huge recorded collections as in Assyria and Alexandriya. There is a tradition about a big library established by the king functioning at Madurai in the Sangam age two thousand years ago. It would not have suddenly come into or went out of existence. There would have been in existence such huge libraries for long time at many places in south India.

Gradually, temples and government entered into the field of education and organization and dissemination of knowledge. Temples became centers of all cultural activities and naturally educational institutions formed part of the temple establishments. When the great centers of advanced learning and their libraries at Nalanda, Vallabhi Vikramasila etc. existed in North, institutions similar to them existed in Kerala. They are commonly called *salas* or *chajas*. Usually they were attached to temples. Most important of them were, Kandaloor Salai, Parthivasekarapuram Salai, Sreevallabapuram Salai, Tiruvalla Salai, Tirunelli Salai and Kottarakkara Salai. Most of them were very much like Post-Graduate Institutions, which imparted higher education in special subjects. Temples met all expenses of education including food and accommodation. Kabdakiir Salai was an ancient institution, the Nalanda of the South and it was looked upon as a model by the people of that time. In Kandaloor Salai even a martial art department was there. It gave training to young who opted For military service. This subjugated the Salai to incessant attacks by Cholas, the enemy kingdom and caused its destruction. There were all facilities for students to get instructions in any subject and proceed by themselves in the higher branches of knowledge. Their collections of manuscripts were vast and varied. The organization and service was efficient. These centres of learning played important part in propagating knowledge and Culture and all these institutions had their libraries, which contained books in all branches of learning which were being copied from time to time.

Professional Status of Libraries

Librarianship was also considered an esteemed profession in ancient Kerala. During the period of the scholar home libraries, and Salais only highly educated persons could work as librarians. The person who kept the documents has to have a very good knowledge about the thought contents of the documents. This tradition of scholar librarians continued upto the medieval period. The copper plate (grant of king Trailokyamalla a Chalukyan ruler, 1058 AD furnishes details of an educational institution maintained by him. It was equipped with a library with six Saraswati Bhandarik (librarians). The inscription further furnishes us details regarding distribution of land, which tells us the dignified and honoured position, the librarians had in temple colleges and other cultural and educational institutions. The importance which the ancient people gave to the collection and dissemination of recorded on the role they assigned to the library in educational process contributed tò the academic excellence of those times, fruits of which are the ancient classics which come to us from those times. Kural, the classified and neatly arranged little work said to be a mustard seed containing the whole universe of knowledge, *Purattirattu* a boók of about 2000 abstracts of all the important works of the South India and many other works which in their way of referencing, footnotes etc. Outshines present day research works took birth at that time due to the merit of the information support system. In modern times such works rarely occur. Any qualitative assessment of contributions to knowledge done during the ancient days, in comparison with the ill reveal that our ancestors were in a higher level than us.

The hundred years war between the Cholas and the Pandays destroyed most of the educational institutions and libraries. Then Aryans who started migrating into Kerala from 8th century slowly gained upper hand in Kerala society. Result was introduction of caste system and loss of access to educational institutions for some classes. The next centuries in which major kingdoms of Kerala took their shape, were full of wars between kings to establish their authorities and mark their boundaries. All that was remaining of the traditional schools, libraries etc. also got disturbed and disappeared.

Free Access to All

Almost all works on history of public libraries considers it an institution of recent origin; that of the nineteenth century. So, there are many arguments against considering, these ancient libraries as public libraries. Mostly ancient libraries existed as part of academic institutions and so we usually classify them under academic libraries. But as we have seen in Kerala's ancient days those libraries were freely open to all and were able to give authentic and efficient information service to the public than our present day public libraries. In our present day also, distance education, which only can reach 75 percent of the common people who cannot approach formal system, is using public libraries as their study centers. So, in all times libraries will inevitably be connected with education. Another argument that ancient libraries were mere storehouses also cannot stand. The fruits of their activity are still lively present in our culture. Then the collections were private, were also not a matter of concern, for as we saw in Kerala's scholar homes they are maintained for the people.

Even in these days of mushroom growth of new institutions, it is the principles of access—as UNESCO defined; open for free and equal use of all members of society—is that which differentiates public library from other libraries. The popular view about the ancient libraries is that they were not accessible to the common people in general. They did not have therefore any direct link with and impact upon lives of the people. But, the study of ancient Kerala's libraries shows that the view is not true. In ancient Kerala education as well as access to houses of recorded knowledge was open to all and there was a hi-fi level of literacy. Acquiring knowledge was not a privilege confined to any class or caste is proved by the fact that scholars of Sangam period were drawn from all walks of life and from all tribes of ancient south. According to an estimate, among the 192 Sangam poets, there were 13 kings, 29 Brahmins, 57 telltales, 36 women, 17 hillmen, 13 foresters, 7 vaniyars, 7 artisans, 1 shepherd, 1 potter etc. Paranar and Kapilar the great Sangam poets of Kerala, and Avvayar belonged to the Pana caste, which is a lower caste in present society. If we consider the present day; 90 percent of the scholars will be from upper strata of society. In ancient days it was not like that. Even female education was not neglected. As a result, we hear several scholarly women who contributed much to the cultural life of their times. *Purananuru* mentions about 15 poetesses by name, most of them belonging to castes now considered inferior. So in ancient Kerala education was more democratic and all the record collections maintained by educational institutions for the whole society.

Origins of Library Legislation

But like the arguments, our limitations in use put against the view of free access to all, to some extent restrictions were there in the access ancient collections and their use. An inscription of Kerala King Karunandakan (857-890 AD) tells us the existence of strict rules inside the Salai's of Kerala. But even in these days, we cannot find any library, without any rules and restrictions. Without some prescribed rules and procedures, no institution can exist. In ancient days, these restrictions were more severe. But they were meant to protect those manuscripts and their information from destruction. Books in the modern sense were unknown and all that those libraries possessed were manuscripts copied with infinite care and patient labour and often at considerable expense. Most of them existed in originals only and if they are lost or destroyed the knowledge stored is also lost forever to the society. So, rules for their preservation and restriction on their use were strictly enforced but judiciously.

They were made available to all those real seekers of that particular thought content. In these ancient customs and rules created and adhered to maximize the utility of those graphic records to society, we find the primitive stages of library legislation. Common customary laws and decrees passed by kings to promote the welfare of the greatest numbers are all legislation in its broad outlook.

Even though, the terms 'library' was not in existence, the social institution, which gathered, preserved and disseminated knowledge existed in Kerala along with the communicating man. They reached their most active period when the scholar homes and Salais existed in Kerala. When we evaluate them giving consideration of the limitations of those times and in comparison with the present state of public libraries in Kerala which we consider progressive, we find that the organization and service of those ancient days were more specialized, efficient, reliable and authentic. They suited the society that created them than the present setup suiting the present day society. Even then as said by Thompson, it is too strange to have to argue that library systems, their basic rules and principles have by and large been established over a very long period of time.

Before the rulers settled after the continuous wars that lasted for hundreds of years for their socio-political and administrative reforms, came the foreign intervention with the landing of VascoDa Gama. Then the French and English followed him. West brought with them their culture, thought, religion and systems that could install them in our land.

As a result, Kerala got an exposure to the specialized library systems of the west. The development in the sociological thought has shattered all the social barriers and forced the society to move towards a socialistic pattern. It implied equal right to all for free public library and information service. It has to be free and supported by legislation because the poorest in the community should get as much that service as the richest. The developments in political thoughts influenced the equal distribution of sovereignty among all adults of the nation through adult franchise. To make this full form of democracy safe and beneficial, it is essential to keep one and all of the citizens furnished with correct information, to provide opportunity for independent judgement on the basis of perusual of all possible views. In its own interest, democracy is obliged to provide free and extensive information service to the people. Industrialization has also made the people's information systems very important. Population pressure has already gone beyond the capacity of the natural and near natural resources to feed, clothe and house all the people. Therefore, there is need for intelligent conservation of all available resources by everybody maximizing the production of natural and near natural commodities by intensive cultivation and the transformation of non-consumable raw materials into beneficial commodities through technology of ever increasing sophistication. These required continuous dissemination of latest scientific ideas and knowledge among one and all of the people. This is development of the human resources of the nation. As the Sangam classic Tirukural, the wealth of all wealth is the wealth of human resources. This makes library and information service the primary responsibility of the state. For the social political and industrial development of a nation, universal education is a necessity. Experience throughout the world has proved that free education for all not backed by free library and information service for all is like a mud house without a roof. Revolutionary changes in Library Concept Knowledge explosion, innovation and speed in printing technology, resultant huge mass of printed materials produced every minute and dependence on information by all aspects of human progress have forced the library to adopt itself quickly and efficiently to these changing situations. Those, which failed to change remained mere curiosity shops.

Through a very fast process of evolution during this century, service oriented libraries of modern world have changed to a state where they are more or less different service outlets, each outlet having the common attitude and approach, common aims and objectives and more or less, uniform organizational and administrative set ups with the whole information resources of the nation at its disposal for dissemination. In this world of fast changing technologies and knowledge explosion, the public library and information service will be futile unless it is organized by staff with proper professional specialization. So, a specialized profession also evolved for this particular work.

In 1927, Kenyon Committee reported that the public interest in libraries has greatly increased and we believe there is now a far healthier belief in the value of knowledge and fill the importance of intellectual life in all busy centres of national activity than in any previous period of history. In such centres the public library is no longer regarded as a means of providing casual recreation of an unimportant character, it is recognized as an engine of great potentialities for national welfare and as an essential foundation for the progress in education and culture without which, no people can hold its own in the struggle for existence.

The developments in the library and information service scene that is fastly achieving new dimensions around the world influenced India also. The movements for evolving, establishing and coordinating library systems in India at the national level and at state level were quickened. A study of the library movement in Kerala in the modern period, which we classify as fifth phase, cannot disregard the direct and indirect influences from these national level movements and the developments in other states. In this chapter, we attempt a brief survey of these developments around Kerala, so that their inter-relationship will become apparent and the library movement in Kerala will appear in perspective as a factor of the developments in the nation as a whole.

Even before India achieved independence, on the part of the Government there were attempts to improve the public information system. Bombay government's attempt to register and support libraries in 1808, Government of India's Press and Registration of Books Act 1867 and the Imperial Library Act of 1902 were some of them.

Baroda Public Library System

Even though Visakam Tirunal Maharaja of Travancore was the first ruler to issue consolidated rules related to all aspects of Public Library System defining the purpose and methods of organizing them, the credit of having initiated the first well articulated system of public libraries under Government order in the Country goes to Sri Sayajirao Gaekward of Baroda State. The Maharaja, an enlightened ruler had in 1906 initiated a scheme of compulsory primary education, the first state in the country to sponsor such a progressive measure. He was of the opinion that the state aided free public libraries are absolutely essential for continuing education. Money spent on few years of compulsory primary education would be of waste unless there is adequate provision for follow up work as a life-long process. Only free public library service can keep the masses literate after their formal education is over. Maharaja linked up primary education with a free public library system as a matter of rule.

The library movement in Baroda started in 1910 when primary education also was made free and compulsory. Maharaja invited Mr. M.A. Borden, an American Librarian in 1910 to introduce a scientifically organized library system. With the assistance of Borden, the Maharaja established the State Central Library and a planned network of free public libraries throughout the State. A first library school was started in 1910 by Borden to train the professionals who are required for running these libraries. A library science journal was also started in 1912. The result of these activities is visible even today in these regions. 85 percent of the people of Baroda have library facilities. But after that Maharaja, there was no follow up work. Maharaja was very much like Sri S.R. Ranganathan, a man ahead of his time and our time also. It took exactly 42 years of struggle in this modern world for Kerala to enact library legislation. Even then it could not envisage a system as efficient as that Baroda have in the beginning of the century. No democratic ruler or Kerala showed a benevolent attitude to this social legislation like Sayajirao.

Kerala Accepts Western Concept of People's Library

It was the alarming increase of illiteracy that led to the intervention of the state in the sphere of education and the formulation of positive educational policy. In Kerala, the direct activity of the state in the field of education began when Her Highness Rani Gouri Parvathi Bal, with the assistance of Col. Munro introduced a system of free and compulsory education under state control in 1817 AD. Maharaja Swathi Tirunal (I 829-1847) a versatile genius and great man of high accomplishments continued these educational reforms. He is considered to be the ruler of Kerala who laid the foundation of modern, system of education in Kerala. In 1830's, English education was recognized as a civilizing agency and government started patronizing the spread of English education by opening English schools. It was he who started in 1836 the first English public school in Travancore. District schools were also started in the same year.

Trivandrum Public Library, 1829

At the beginning of nineteenth century, in Kerala also there was no institution with the name public library. The first public library and the oldest of its kind in India came into existence during Swathi Tirunal's reign. The then British resident of Travancore was Col. Edward Cadogan. Cadogan was the grandson of Sir Hans Sloans, the founder of the British

Museum and he could very easily make the Maharaja and high officials aware of the need and modern education system. Swathy Tirunal was also a great scholar, ill many languages a poet, a musician, and a musical composer of very high order. He was easily impressed by the idea of an institution like British Museum joining together they established in 1829 the Trivandrum Public Library. The king took active interest in the affairs of the public library throughout his reign. An association called Trivandrum Public Library Committee of which the British Resident was the president first managed the library. In 1889, the Trivandrum Public Library Committee entered into an agreement with the Government according to which their entire assets were handed over to the Govemment. The condition was that the Government would erect a suitable building for a new library for the benefit of the public and to that end provide a well stocked furnished reference library and should undertake the maintenance of the same in a suitable manner under such regulations as may be best calculated to carry out the end in view. Accordingly Government took over the management of Trivandrum Public Library and it was treated as one of the minor departments of the state. The British Resident continued to serve as the president of the committee.

Education and Libraries in Cochin

In Cochin, the Government undertook the responsibility of educating the people in 1818 when the first state owned schools were started there. District schools were started in 1877. Christian Missionaries also established many educational institutions in different parts of Travancore, Cochin and Malabar area. In the later half of the nineteenth century, Governments of Travancore and Cochin began to patronize English education at higher levels and so opened a lot of English schools and colleges. The first college was started in 1875. In all these educational institutions, very efficient library services were also organized on the pattern of library service available in Britain. The teachers and library staff were usually Britishers at the beginning. The producers of these educational institutions realized the value of libraries. They took initiative in influencing the rulers to establish libraries in different parts of the country so that libraries will be accessible to them in then public life also.

Government supported public libraries were established at Ernakulam in 1869, Trichur in 1873, Kottayam in 1881, Tellichery in 1901, Calicut in 1924 and Cannanore in 1927. These libraries continuously maintained good collections and services upto 1950's.

Library Awareness

Social and political activists who used the services of established libraries by Government became aware of the wide possibilities of such institutions. Spread of education and the birth of a large number of newspapers and journals in the state and the revolutions that were going on in the social and Political spheres of life kindled in the people, a desire to have such public libraries very near to them so that they can also get the daily news and discuss on them. All these contributed to the birth of a people's 'library movement in the end of the nineteenth century which we have to discuss as the next phases.

Government supported and nourished the people's movement. But at the same time, Government continued its own independent projects of library development resulting in two parallel movements in the regions of library field. Governments contributions strictly adhered to some generally accepted library principles, which were static throughout next three phases. It is very much like an extension of second phase through later phases and so we have to discuss those developments here itself to avoid confusion.

Initiation of Modern Library Legislation

The State Government was continuously active in library affairs. It was aware of its responsibility to establish and maintain library and information services for the people. During the reign of Sri Moolam Tirunal Maharaja of Travancore rules were framed to give grant-in-aid to libraries for the first time. The rules were published in Travancore Gazette in 1918. The conditions prescribed by this rule for a library to be eligible for grant are:

> The libraries should be under the administrative control of a committee or officials recognized or appointed by the Director of Education. The reading facilities in the library must be open to all free of cost. No restrictions based on caste or religion should be imposed on its users. The rules of the library or reading room should be approved by the Director of Education. The accounts, registers and records should be maintained in a proper way and must be supplied for verification to the Assistant Inspector of Elementary Schools when ever he calls for them.

The rules also prescribed some minimum standards related to the collection to be maintained, services to be done etc. and explained the procedures for fixing the rate of annual grants, and grants for construction of building, and purchase of furniture and equipments. It also sanctioned the issue of government publications free of cost or at reduced rates to these libraries.

These rules framed by the Government in its own initiative contain the basic objectives of public library and the most important factors of modern library legislation. In these rules, Government accepted that libraries are also educational institutions which have to play a role equal to that of schools and colleges, in education. The rules accepts that it was Government's responsibility to establish and maintain library service for the public. The unique feature of the rules was its acceptance that public library service must be a free service to the public. The reading and consultation facilities are to be made available to the public free of cost by all the libraries that get Government grant. It was only from the later half of the nineteenth century that social forces worked towards free book service for all, even in western countries. Providing totally free library service to the public is yet an ideal to be realized even in the states which have enacted legislation including the present day Kerala where this law was in force in those old days. Free supply of Government publications to libraries was also a progressive move provided in these rules.

Libraries for the Spread of Education

Government took the encouragement of libraries as a part of its programme for expansion of educational facilities in the state. Before 1928 Government has established a number of libraries especially for the use of women. The Travancore Educational Reform Committee under the Chairmanship of RM Statham, in 1932 made certain recommendations regarding the development of public libraries in order to advance education and to provide facilities for adult education. Immediate action followed. The Director of Public Instruction was asked to prepare a scheme and accordingly he prepared a scheme for establishment of a central circulating library and a large number of rural libraries. In 1935 the Government sanctioned the opening of sixty such rural libraries attached to departmental primary schools in important underdeveloped areas of the state. Government feared that literate people would lapse into illiteracy unless reading and study can be practiced with the aid of libraries in these regions. Provision was made for each library to receive a particular number of periodicals and newspapers. The system gradually developed into 354 libraries with an average of 500 selected standard books and 42 newspapers and periodicals.

In Cochin also, parallel development was going on during this period. The Government of Cochin began to establish experimental village libraries since 1926 in various parts of the state to support its program of adult education. In 1946, there were three types of libraries. Seventeen public libraries, five major rural libraries and more than five hundred village libraries. The annual expenditure for library development in the state during 1947-49 was Rs. fifty thousands.

State Central Library

The Trivandrum Public Library run directly by the government from 1888 was transferred to the control of the University of Travancore in 1938. A new committee was constituted by Government with Pro-Vice-Chancellor as the president and the University Librarian as secretary. The committee had full powers to manage the affairs of the institution and to approve all expenditures. But this transfer of institution met with resentments and protests from the library conscious public, and newspapers published editorials and a number of articles against this order. The apprehension was that, following the transfer of the library to the control of the university; the library may not be accessible to the public as before and the usefulness of the rich collection might be reduced, restricted and limited. The concern of the public expressed through newspapers and in some cultural functions during this period vindicated one thing. In the preceding half century during which it was a direct department of government, the library has served the public very efficiently. The discontinuation or chance in its service was too disheartening to the literate public.

Due to this forceful public opinion, a resolution was unanimously passed by the legislature in 1948. It resolved that Government should take over the institution from the university and manage it as a separate department as was done upto 1938. Accordingly, the Government resumed the control of the institution in 1949. The committee was also reconstituted with the Minister for Education as President and the Librarian as the convener of the committee. The committee continued to be in charge of the management of the library. In 1956, Government included this library in the plan scheme and sanctioned about seven lakhs rupees for converting the library into State Central Library and the District Distributing Library for Trivandrum. A State Librarian was also appointed. To increase the libraries usefulness and to extend its services, half a dozen libraries from the northern border to the southern border of the state were affiliated to it within two years.

Local Library Authorities

Malabar region which formed part of the Madras State and which came to Kerala with the re-organization of states had in 1956 about 500 libraries excluding those run by Local Library Authority under the provisions of Madras Library Act. Local Library Authorities were constituted in 1951 for the whole of Malabar. The Calicut Municipal Library with a large collection of books was converted into District Central namely Calicut, Cannanore and Palghat. So, three Local Library Authorities started functioning in 1959 according to the provisions of Madras Public Library Act. Recently, Kasaragod and Malappuram Districts were formed dividing Cannanore and Calicut. In each district, local library authority has a district central library at district headquarters and branch libraries under it.

Rules and Standards

In 1959, Government issued an order constituting a State Library Advisory Board. The Board consisted fifteen members with Minister for Education as Chairman, Director of Public Instruction as Secretary and State Librarian ex-officio member. The functions of the Board were to formulate rules related to libraries and advise the Government on the affairs of the libraries and the Kerala Granthasala Sangham. Through an order issued in 1958 the Government channelised the disbursement of grants to rural libraries through District Education Officers.

Another order concerning the grant for construction of library buildings and purchase of equipments made the libraries strictly adhere to the approved designs published with that order, for building and equipments. In 1996, Government decided to continue a system of grant in aid to libraries until a Library Act could be passed. The various rules and orders relating to the payment of grant to libraries were consolidated by a Government Order. This order made provisions for, annual grant to libraries, building and furniture, annual grant to Granthasala Sangham and allowances to librarians. In 1971 Government constituted a gradation committee, which tour throughout the state and review and report about the libraries receiving grant 1976 and 1981 Government issued orders classifying the libraries into six grades and fixing the different rates of their annual grants.

Movement of the People

In Kerala, influenced by the British, the Government contributed much to the growth and modernization of libraries than anywhere else in India continuously throughout nineteenth and twentieth centuries. In library field, Kerala is also known for a century old people's library movement. It was a unique movement in its nature and growth. It has a spontaneous growth from the minds of the people. It grew parallel to the library development projects of the State.

Various social and political forces directly or indirectly contributed to the birth and growth of people's library movement. The second half of the nineteenth century witnessed the full flowering of national political consciousness and the growth of an organized national movement in India. This resulted in recognizing the increased importance of the individual. Creating public opinion and spreading political ideas warranted an educated and informed public. Political workers therefore gave more emphasis to social education activities including the establishment of public libraries. The people's library movement got special impetus, also from the emergence of political parties social reform movements, communal and religious organizations and the struggle for responsible government in the State.

Political and Social Reformation

The spread of western education influenced movements for social and political reform in Kerala from the end of nineteenth century. Rulers of Kerala were benevolent and modern in out look. So most of the people's movements were bloodless revolutions that reaped victory. The Maharaja of Travancore set up the first legislature in any Indian State in 1888. Three years later representatives of the slowly growing middle class presented to the king a memorial known as Malayale Memorial, signed by more than 10000 persons. It appealed to the king to give a share to the people in the administration of the State, which was then largely done by persons imported from Madras. This agitation continued for a decade. It awakened the middle class of Travancore to a sense of their inherent rights, thereby paving the way for a new chapter in the political history of the State.

In all the communities in Kerala, from the highest to the lowest in social strata; obsolete customs and practices were alive during nineteenth century. The western educated and progressive minded younger generation started reform activities and resisted outdated customs, traditions and systems of inheritance, succession and family organization.

National Movement

Freedom movement also developed the spirit of library movement in Kerala. In 1903, Indian National Congress held a large public meeting at Calicut under the chairmanship of a veteran congress leader C. Vijaya Raghavacharyar. In 1910, a branch of the famous Home Rule League, Mrs. Annie Besant was formed in Malabar. Civil Disobedience Movement of 1930 and 1932-33 and regional social movements like Guruvayoor Temple Satyagraha for permitting the lower caste people to enter into the temple stirred the Kerala society, peasants, workers, teachers and many other groups became organized and were drawn into politics. In the forties besides Quit India Movement, the agitation for self-government in Travancore and Cochin States gathered momentum. In Travancore, the Travancore State Congress and in Cochin, the Cochin Praja Mandalam led the movement. The common culture, language, literature and the parallel social and political reform movements going on in the States of Kerala, Cochin and Malabar and the spread of national movement quickly gave birth to the idea of a United Kerala by the dissolution of the political boundaries which kept them as distinct political units.

Seeds of People's Library Movement

It was the newspapers and the curiosity for the daily news that prompted the speedy establishment of thousands of village libraries in a very short period. Writings of Mahatma Gandhi and other leaders of the national movement exercised tremendous influence on the people. The persons who undertook leadership in social and political reform movements in Kerala read and translated those works into regional language.

In Kerala during the days of the national movement, the persons belonging to the congress socialist party, which developed within the congress, took active interest in cultural renaissance. They knew that political and literary works, dramas and discussions were the best mediums used throughout the world to educate the public, to rouse their political and social consciousness and to kindle the fire of revolutions. The result was a progressive literature movement. A flood of novels, dramas and poems dealing with social, political and economic issues appeared. They were produced with the intention of creating an awareness of their rights among the peasant workers and lower middle class and to infuse into them the thought of the need to fight for their rights. But majority of people remained beyond the reach of these mediums due to literacy, poverty and lack of communication systems. So, the political and social, reformers searcher for venues closest to the people from where almost a natural dialogue with the common people can become possible. Their search ended in the venues or institutions that were public libraries. Many public libraries like Trivandrum Public Library established by Government were functioning satisfactorily, disseminating knowledge, news and ideas to the people. Already, the people with their own initiative established many libraries on this model. The first attempt by the people to establish such an institution was during the reign of Visakam Tirunal Maharaja. With his support a library named Suguna Poshini was established in 1880 at Vanchiyoor Trivandrum and a vast collection of Malayalam books was organized there. The SRMV association Library at Karamana started functioning in 1888. Jnanapradayini Library of Neyyattinkara, Sankara Vilasam Library of Clieiit-,atitioor and Cliltliti—a Tiruiial Siiiaraka Graiitliasala of Trivandrum came into existence before 1920 due to people's initiative. All these libraries conducted literary and cultural activities and discussions on topics of current interest. The contributions of Clilthira Tirunal Smarak—a Granthasala of Vanchiyoor to Kerala culture and literature was enormous. For almost six decades, it functioned in close association with the most notable cultural and literary figures. Popularization of standard literature and arts done by this institution was to a remarkable extent.

Venues to Spread Reform Movements

The political and social activists found in these libraries their base, the nucleus in society from where they can spread their reform movements and activities. With this motive they involved or infiltrated in the existing people's libraries. They used them and also established thousands of new libraries in the places where they were not already available. The Congress and Communist workers organized in them study circles, evening classes, adult education programmes etc. The novels, poems and essays of the progressive literary movement were usually circulated through these libraries. Their dramas which discussed the social, political and economic problems, produced with the intention of attracting and retaining more workers of the national movement and for formally public opinion were staged in connection with the programmes organized by these libraries. Enormous quantity of reading materials discussing the political and social problems, published by the political parties, communal organizations, trade unions, youth associations, women's organization etc. flowed into these village libraries. The increased use of the libraries and reading rooms has raised them to the level of cultural centers of the localities. This tendency was more noticeable in the rural areas and therefore apparently the villages were the beneficiaries. In fact these libraries and reading rooms attained almost the position occupied by temples in medieval Kerala. They were similar to the scholar homes and Salais we came upon in the ancient Kerala in few aspects. The depth of the knowledge activity, the ancient institutions have had the new ones lacked. But the inviting atmosphere was present here also.

Such a long, continuous and live involvement of State and the people in library affairs is a rare phenomena. The concept followed by the State in library development was establishing and maintaining public libraries in all places as independent self-sufficient units. State also fully supported people's move for establishing and maintaining such units almost independent of state control. When the western concept of each public library as service outlet of a library and information dissemination system for the people took birth State tried to establish such a system and it resulted in the Kerala Public Library Act of 1989.

References

Achutha Menon. *Cochi Rajyacharitham*. Calicut: Mathrubhoomi, 1989.

Dunlap, Leslie W. *Readings in Library History*. London: RR Bowker, 1972.

Gopinath, M.A. Madras. In Ranganathan *op. cit.*, 9.

Gopnatha Rao, Ed. *Travancore archeological series*. Vol. 1, Trivandrum: Government Press, 1947.

Hessel, Alfred. A history of libraries. Translated by Reuben Peiss. Washington: Scare Crow, 1977.

Kerala Legislature, Secretariat of Kerala Public Library Bill 1971: Background materials. Trivandrum: The Author 1972.

Kunjan Pillai, Elamkulam PN. Studies in Kerala history, Kottayam: NBS, 1970.

Nilakanta Sastri, KA. History of South India from prehistoric times to present, London: OUP, 1959.

Olle, James G. Library history, London: CliveBingley, 1967.

Panikar, P.N. Ed. Keralathile Granthasala Prasthanam. Trivandrum: State Gazetters, 1986, Vol. 2, Part 1.

Raman Nair. R. Public library development in Kerala: a historical perspective.

Proceedings of South Indian History Congress. Dharwad, Karnataka University, 1992.

Raman Nair, R. Public Library Systems in Ancient South India. II.A Bulletin, Vo. 12 No.3, 1991.

Raman Nair, R. National Library: A historical perspective . International Library Movement, 1987, Vol. 9, No. 1.

Ranganathan, S.R. Free book service for all: An International Survey. Bombay: Asia, 1968.

Sreedhara Menon, Ed. Kerala District Gazetteers: Trivandrum. Trivandrum: Govt. Press, 1962.

Thompson, James, History of Principles of librarianship. London: Clive Bingley, 1977.

Travancore Gazette No.39, Education sheet, 9th Kanni 1093 ME (1918 AD) Trivandrum: Government Press.

Travancore-Cochin. Government Order No. M 98 dated 5.2.1958.

Trivandrum Public Library. Administration report. Trivandrum: Government Press, 1981.

Velu Pillai. T.K. *Travancore state manual*. Trivandrum: Government Press, 1947.

12

Representing Culture, Repossessing History: Cultural Nuances in Three Indian English Novels

Usha Bande

"The schoolmaster is abroad, and I trust more to him, armed with his primer, than I do the soldier in full military array, for upholding and extending the liberties of his country."

Lord Brougham in a speech in the House of Commons, 29 Jan. 1929

Cultural implication of the colonial experience is one of the significant aspects of literature studies in the post-colonial period. The main preoccupation of the literature of the erstwhile-colonized countries has been to resist the imperial myths and fallacies by writing back to the center. The effort is to preserve one's self-image and establish an indigenous identity. As Franz Fanon opines, colonialism not only enslaves a people politically, it devalues their pre-colonial history and invades their culture. The victims of this historical process suffer loss of identity and undergo psychological conflicts. In the post-colonial era, therefore, the urgent need of the society is to re-possess its past and take control of its own reality by "charting the cultural territory," to use Edward Said's words. In literature this is termed as *reinscription* (Said 1994: 252-59). What Said asserts in his *Culture and Imperialism* is that though identity is crucial to the post-colonial, it is not enough to define it as "a different identity" (257). The important thing is to be able to see and show others that even the subaltern has had a history capable of development, as part of the process of growth and maturity. That is where re-writing or reinscription assumes significance. While some Indian critics see post-colonial theory of literature as "ideologically an emancipatory concept" given to a "rigorous scrutiny on the continuities and ruptures in the de-colonized societies" (Mukherjee 1996: 3), some others question its efficacy and efficiency for the Indian situation. These critics feel that though the post-colonial literature tends to write back to the center it does not solve the question of marginality. Post-colonialism, Jasbir Jain asserts is a "question of attitude which goes beyond the attempt to confront colonialism to become an attempt to transcend it, to step outside the influence and the framework, to reclaim an autonomous and free identity" (Jain 1999:35).

In this paper, an attempt has been made to study three Indian English novels to see how the authors reclaim their identity by re-mapping their cultural territory and how by reverting to the traditional narrative strategies they work out an indigenous framework. The novels selected for discussion are Arun Joshi's *The City and the River* (1990), *The Last Labyrinth* (1981), and Gita Mehta's *A River Sutra* (1993). The discussion will focus on the narratives, analyzing the cultural consciousness of the authors, which shapes their texts. In these stories, the Ganga, the Narmada and the Himalayas are the bearers of the culture, witness to a historical reality and the repository of ancient wisdom. The novels show the authors' cultural efforts to restore the community and repossess the culture. Both Joshi and Mehta uphold the cultural dynamism of traditional thought and hold a mirror to the destructive trends in power politics and consumerism-oriented greed. The fictional narratives, by re-creating an indigenous culture displace the historical discourse and help us read into the text the mythological, archetypal, metaphysical and religious perception in the native literature.

Arun Joshi's *The Last Labyrinth* was published in 1981. A Sahitya Akademy award winning work, this novel recounts the story of a modern Indian town between the inner and the outer forces, the instinctive cultural leaning of the inner self and the rational, scientific yet consumer orientation of a Westernized Indian. The shares of Aftab's Company that Som Bhaskar desperately wants to grab are in the possession of Krishna in a temple on the Himalayas. Som's greed makes him undertake the difficult journey up the mountain, through the formidable crags and valleys, the glaciers and the frozen lakes; he dreads it, it is nightmarish but he is fascinated by it, all the same. As the author describes the mission one realizes that the Himalayas and Lord Krishna assume significance as cultural symbols. Som broods with a kind of cultural pride and admits unabashedly, "No, there is nothing simple about Krishna. Had it been so. He would not have survived ten thousand years. He would have died long ago with the gods of the Pharaohs, the Sumerians, Incas. Krishna was about as simple as the labyrinth of Aftab's Haveli" (Joshi 1981:173). Som's journey through the Himalayas is reminiscent of the last climb of the Pandavas commonly known as *Swarga-rohan;* only, Som lacks attitudinal change; he tosses between an urge for self-understanding and the inability to forget his recent past and consequently his journey becomes one of nightmares, unfulfilled desires and failure. For a brief while, Som gets a kind of illumination, a short spell of peak experience that could have transformed him into a self-realized man, but as he admits, "This little flame of mine...yielded nothing beyond an ounce of tranquility" (p. 209). Throughout the climb, we are not allowed to forget that it is the Himalayas the protagonist is climbing up on. Symbolically, his companions are Doctor K. and a friend called Vasudeva. K. could be read as an abbreviation for Krishna while Vasudeva is one of the many names of Lord Krishna. Thus, the journey assumes obvious cultural overtones. The author juxtaposes the puniness of man with the vastness of the unfathomable. The entire fabric of the narrative is dominated by the author's efforts to reclaim the culture and the inability to revert to the past.

In his last novel *The City and the River*, published in 1990, Arun Joshi deals with the existential anguish of the entire culture. It is a muffled portrayal of post-independence India, a kind of allegorical picture, where intrigues, nepotism, ostracism and violence are rampant. The regime of the Grand Master in a particular city is full of fawning sycophants, self-seeking ruling classes and the helpless, hapless masses. The scenario, in fact, draws parallel between the Emergency in India and the oppressive regime of the Grand Master. The city becomes the victim of the greed of the purblind rulers and is destroyed by the angry river. The 'City' is unnamed and so is the 'River' but both gain multi-dimensional meanings when read in the national and cultural context. The narrative pattern of story within a story told by an old, wise teacher to his keen disciple follows the typical Indian narrational technique of *Katha*. In the Indian narrative tradition, a *sutradhar* or the main narrator recounts a story with the help of which the story (or the novel in the present case) advances. Often the framed stories are variations of some broad human behaviour. *Panchtantra, Kadambari, Katha Sarit Sagar*, and even epics like the *Mahabharata* and the *Ramayana*, and a whole lot of our traditional narratives follow the pattern of "framed narrative".

In *The City and the River*, the Great Yogeshwara tells the story to the Nameless-One. After giving enlightenment to his disciple in the 'Prologue' the teacher, the Guru, starts thus: "That is good. I shall tell you now a tale and in my telling perhaps, you will know who you are. Listen, this is how it goes"(11). The story starts with the chapter entitled 'The Grand Master's Dream' and ends with the city's doom. Then follows the 'Epilogue'. Again the teacher-pupil duo appears. The novel ends but not the cycle of comings and goings. The Nameless-One has been entrusted with the task of purifying the city "of egoism, selfishness, stupidity" (p. 263). The cyclical movement is thus inevitable: "On the ruins of that city ...a new city has risen. It is ruled by another Grand master," it has the same people—Professor, Bhumiputra, the boatmen and so on. Of course, the men have "other names but the forces they embody remain unchanged" (p. 262). The Great Yogeshawara wants his disciple to try and "prevent this endless repetition, this periodic disintegration" (p. 262). The circular movement communicates human continuity. The Indian concept of life-death-reincarnation implies the cycle from creation to the end and again a new beginning. The reappearance of the Nameless-One signifies a period of future hope for humanity.

The third novel I propose to discuss is Gita Mehta's *A River Sutra*. A retired Administrative Officer decides to renounce the world and stay in a secluded spot. He gets a job as the manager of Narmada Guest House and during the course of his stay, he learns much about life through interaction with Tariq Mia and the others who frequent the guest house. Gita Mehta also adopts the traditional Indian narrational technique. Its oral tradition of mythologizing is a well-chosen device that makes the novel gripping and convincing. The several threads of narrative run parallel with the main story and are held together by the frame narrator. Each tale, narrated from the point of view of some specific narrator, be it the diary of Nitin Bose or the first person tale of the courtesan/monk, is discussed by the frame-narrator. The analysis and the comments bear upon the limits of human understanding. The novelist seems to have consciously evoked the Guru-Shishya (teacher-pupil) dialogue on the pattern of the Upanishadic framework. In the beginning of the novel the bureaucrat-narrator says: "Do you know what the word Upanishad means? It means to sit beside and listen. Here I am, sitting eager to listen" (13). While Joshi's novel *The City and the River* has third person narrator, Gita Mehta shifts between the device of first person and third-person narrative strategy, according to the exigency of the story. In Joshi's novel, the Great Yogeshwara tells one long tale of human greed and shameful actions and lets the 'river' take its revenge; in *A River Sutra* there are six isolated stories all joined by common threads: at the human level by Tariq Mia and/or the bureaucrat-narrator, at the archetypal level by river Narmada, and at the metaphysical level by the bonds of human love which lead to divine love. The movement of this novel is linear, meandering like the river but going forward. The Narmada has a life of its own—the pilgrims on its banks, the dancing waters eager to join the sea, the aquatic life inside the river, and the whirling eddies. The river is a living force with a personality. It is a delightful river. Joshi's river, on the other hand, can be angry, incomprehensible, and vindictive. Within these structural patterns, though alike to an extent but different still, the two novelists weave stories deeply rooted in the culture. Both join the contemporary India with the ageless, immortal India; the present with the past, the modern with the traditional, the mythic with the rational.

The nameless river in Joshi's novel is the archetypal symbol of the great mother. It is interesting to note that the novel does not have any memorable female presence except the 'River'. True, the "headman" of the boat people is a woman but she is not a feminine figure, she is an abstract concept. There is Shailaja, but she fails to be a palpable presence. Only the river is the moving loving, protecting force to whom the boat people owe allegiance. For them the river is a symbol of the living mother. Of God himself (P. 22). The rational, modern and consumer mind of the Grand Master is not ready to accept this superstition. He tells the Astrologer, "it is these things that keep our people down" (P. 22), because to him what is the river but a stream of water. That the boatmen should have allegiance to the river than to their Ruler is beyond his comprehension. "They prefer a stream of water, no doubt beautiful, no doubt sacred, but nonetheless a stream, to me, the scion of a family that gives all to this city" (P. 22). The boatmen consider themselves children of the river, their archetypal mother, the harbinger of peace and plenty. This tussle is a pointer towards the conflict going on in contemporary India - fast moving towards Western rational approach yet tied down to the unconscious, to the old beliefs. Joshi carries the question to the end of the novel when it assumes philosophical proportion and becomes a treatise on the question of man's allegiance "to God or to man" (p. 262).

The answer to this question can be found in *A River Sutra* when the Naga Baba alias Prof. Shankar asserts towards the end, dismissing the divinity of river Narmada, "if anything is sacred about the river, it is the individual experiences of the human beings who have lived here" (p. 267). Suddenly then, a reader returns to the epigram from the "Love Songs of Chandidas":

> Listen, O brother,
> Man is the greatest truth.
> Nothing beyond.

The novel, we realize, affirms human dignity. Narmada becomes a palpable symbol of love, life, and death. Born of Shiva's penance, the river is the "Delightful one, forever holy, forever inexhaustible." To Prof. Shankar, it is an "immortal river", while for Nitin Bose and the tribals it has curative value. Narmada grants salvation to those who die in its water. Suicide is not a sin if committed in Narmada. And, the river sustains love and teaches the lover not to be moved by the puny human passions but to see love as sublime. This is corroborated by the story of the musician who exhorts his daughter to "meditate on the waters of Narmada, the symbol of Shiva's penance," until she has cured herself of her attachment to what has passed in her life. The father exhorts his daughter to understand that she is "the bride of music, not of a musician..." (p. 226). The tale of Naga Baba's love for the child he rescues from the brothel and gives a clean life, is humanistic/philanthropic, while the music teacher's attachment to the blind boy is love at the level of Guru-Shishya tradition. The aesthetic framework moves round love, attachment-detachment, renunciation and involvement. Apart from these, there are rich motifs of divine love—the reference to Kama, allusion to Parvati's penance to get Shiva's love, the stories about Veena and the seven notes of music uphold the divinity of love. Gita Mehta quotes profusely from the great Sufi poet Rumi's love lyrics strengthening the images of love as a purifying emotion, above the narrow worldly barriers. In Joshi's *The Last Labyrinth*, Gargi exhorts Som time and again to consider his love for Anuradha on the spiritual plain. Could Som get over the physicality of his passion for Anuradha he would have been saved the torture of schizophrenia after Anuradha's disappearance. Som comes to realize the pure quality of love during his trip to the Himalayas but unfortunately for him he is unable to assimilate the lesson.

In *The City and The River*, Arun Joshi presents predominantly modern India scourged by self-seeking, shortsighted, lusty and power-hungry ruling classes. In *The Last Labyrinth*, he focuses on the greed and lust of an individual character. But in his scheme, there exists a greater, perennial India with its eternal wisdom. The clash of tradition and modernity, rationality and instinct will always be there. What is required is purification. This, however, is hard to achieve. The City is symbolic of the contemporary society. It is the inert battleground of power play. In *The Last Labyrinth*, Som seeks the power of money and passionate love in Benaras while in *The City and The River*, the Rulers of the unnamed City want unquestioned political power. The River is a primordial force to which all turn for help. In her anger, she becomes destructive though she is not life denying. On her bosom the Nameles-One is born to continue creation, life and its eternal quest. Taken as an Indian archetype, the river appears to be Ganga. In *The Last Labyrinth* also, it is Ganga at Benaras on whose waters Som is ferried to Gargi's place.

Gita Mehta's Narmada too is a microcosm of India. She is the organizing principle of the novel. The six loosely knit tales give the novel multiplicity but the river vouchsafes its unity. "The resulting figure", as a critic observes, "is one of unitary pluralism". The Narmada Guest House is, indeed, mini-India and it reflects her culture. Here is the river with its mythology, religion, superstitions, spirituality and archaeology, representing traditional, primitive and modern India. People who converge around the area come from different walks of life and belong to different religious groups. The Narmada joins the north and the south. Its legends are as much known to the tribals in Assam as to the tribals of the Vano village. The pre-Aryan and the Aryan cultures prevail. It is thus a secular river. If the traditional wisdom chants: "O Narmada defend me from the serpent's poison," the rational mind interprets it as the "serpent of desire"; if it stings, the result would be schizophrenic state, symbolized by Nitin Bose in the novel and Som Bhaskar in Joshi's work.

The three novels do not advocate detachment in the sense of running away from life, from action. Naga Baba enters the battlefield of life, "Kurukshetra", after ten years of ascetic wandering. Tariq Mia makes himself socially useful by teaching his students. He is content with his life. The music teacher was attached to his blind pupil; this led him to grief and suicide. The significant thing is to maintain balance. Non-attachment is difficult, as the ugly daughter of the musician says, "It is an impossible penance, to express desire in my music when I am dead inside" (p. 226). But, it is worth trying as Naga Baba alias Prof. Shankar shows.

The novels under discussion are the authors' cultural efforts at the restoration of community and repossession of culture. The city in *The Last Labyrinth* is Benaras, the cultural city of India; it is not the colonial city of which Sunil Khilnani speaks in *The Idea of India*. The significance of Indian cities is given in a *shloka*, which refers to seven cities as *mokshadayini*. The Shloka runs thus:

> Ayodhya, Mathuramaya, Kashi, Kanchi, Avantika,
> Puri, Dwarawatishchaiva saptehta mokshdayika.

Now, coming to the rivers, to the Indian mind, rivers are not only the geographical features; they are the very sum and substance of our existence. We have mythologized our rivers, given them a form and a life of their own. They are timeless, ageless and immutable on whose banks life has continued for ages and ages. They sustain and purify, give us joy, and in anger, they can even destroy, only to create again. Thus, hope is sustained; culture springs up around them and philosophy, religion, mythology, archaeology take roots. One cannot forget Lord Krishna's frolicking in and around the Yamuna so lovingly described in the literature of India; one is reminded of the Saryu of the Ramayana, Kalidas's Kshipra, the place of Godavari and Kaveri in the psyche of the South, the power of the Brahmaputra (the only male) and the love and awe attached to the five rivers of the Punjab. As for the Himalayas, it is a part of the unconscious of the race. In the *Gita*, Lord Krishna calls himself Himalayas among the mountains.

Discussing the process of de-colonization Edward Said remarks: "After the period of 'primary resistance', literally fighting against outside intrusion, there comes a period on secondary, that is, ideological resistance"(1994:252-53), when efforts are made to reconstitute a community and restore its dignity and unity. By this process the subaltern occupies his place self-consciously so as to gain his rightful place. Said gives examples from literature to make his point. Ngugi induces life in the river Honia in *The River Between* and Tayb Salih re-maps the power of the

Nile in *Season of Migration*. When compared to Conrad's river in the *Heart of Darkness*, the above two rivers—Honia and Nile—appear living entities. Only an insider who has imbibed the culture with his/her mother's milk can think of nationalism in terms of cultural practices (254-55).

Both Gita Mehta and Arun Joshi suggest a rethinking of Indian culture and tradition. Joshi hints at the self-destructive trends of the power politics and warns contemporary India. He advocates purity of thought and action through the story of the city and the river, and through Som's dissipation. Gita Mehta weighs the mysticism of *Vanprastha* in the scale of modern rationality and finds that the dynamism of Indian thought has always advocated detachment with action, and animism with humanism. The self-contained and interconnected characters and tales reconcile the rich diversity of doctrines in the flow of Narmada—the symbol of our cultural multiplicity and unity. The Narmada guest house is symbolic of this world where people come, stay awhile and depart. This oriental view reminds us of Omar Khayyam's Rubayyat likening this world to a "Caravan Sarai". The bureaucrat manager of the guesthouse represents the modern seeker—confused and unable to decide what to choose: this world or *Vanaprastha*. He is knowledgeable but his knowledge is pre-eminently in the shape of information, not wisdom. As Tariq Mia often says teasingly, one has yet to learn a lot about the world before one seeks renunciation.

At the end of Mehta's novel, the bureaucrat seeker broods as the river goes on and the lamps glittering on the current indicate a ray of hope for the soul marching for merger in the Higher Being. In Joshi's *The City and the River*, the river overwhelms a complete civilization yet it is a benevolent force because on its water floats the hope of a new life, of a new beginning. In *The Last Labyrinth*, the Himalaya, the Ganga, and Varanasi vouchsafe soothing, purifying effect but one has to get rid of the puny passions and desires if one wants to achieve self-actualization. The images created by the authors and the significance of the images in their respective contexts can be safely studied in the light of the present imperatives. In his *Nation and Narration*, Homi Bhabha points out that a nation is a cultural space representing certain events at every point of time that change and with it changes the image. But the myths and the archetypes grant the culture of that nation continuity, and a creative writer by his dexterous handling of these mythical frameworks and the synchronization of individual history with the national history reflect the social concerns and becomes the beacon light. By reverting to the cultural past, Arun Joshi and Gita Mehta subtly draw from the perennial past and give momentum to both the literary culture and history.

References

Bhabha, Homi K. *The Nation and Narration*. London: Routledge, 1997.

Fanon, Franz. *The Wretched of the Earth*. New York: Mentor Books, 1969.

Jain, Jasbir. "Interpreting the Past: Culture and History in Sahgal's Works." Surya Nath.

Pandey. Ed. *Writing in a Post Colonial Space*. New Delhi: Atlantic, 1999.

Joshi, Arun. *The Last Labyrinth*. New Delhi: Orient Paperbacks, 1981.

____. *The City and The River*. New Delhi: Vision Books, 1990.

Khilnani, Sunil. *The Idea of India*. London: Hamish Hamilton, 1997.

Mehta, Gita. *A River Sutra*. New Delhi: Penguin, 1993.

Mukherjee, Meenakshi. "Interrogating Post-Colonialism," Harish Trivedi and Meenakshi Mukherjee, Ed. *Interrogating Post-Colonialism: Theory, Text and Context. Shimla*: Indian Institute of Advanced Study, 1997.

Said, Edward. *Imperialism and Culture*. London: Vintage, 1994.

13

Theatre of Protest in Kerala

Vayala Vasudevan Pillai

The element of protest has been very active in Kerala Theatre during the last forty years, particularly in the seventies and eighties. The upsurge was felt in every walk of life and theatre eloquently expressed this new wave of rejuvenation. It was part of the renaissance movement triggered off by the revolutionary and social activists like Shri Narayana Guru, Dr. Palpu, V.T. Bhattathirippad, K. Kelappan, E.M. Sankaran Namboodirippad and many others. All these pioneers in their own ways struck new channels of creative expression challenging the stagnant values of the past. It was in a way, a movement of liberation, freeing the spirit of man imprisoned by social norms, customs and practices. The struggle for liberation manifested itself in terms of politics, religion and economics in all walks of life. It shattered the centres of power and theatre became a powerful instrument for social mobilization and protest.

The theatre of protest in Kerala provides an in-depth study of how the oppressed has been struggling hard through decades to liberate the strength locked up in him. It is a study of the structural conflicts latent in our society. The man who was deprived of his right and dignity as an individual in society sought to make himself heard and listened to. In the traditional theatre of Kerala, his role was that of only a witness. The Sanskrit, Parsi and the Western influences, whether separately or collectively, defined for the theatre enthusiast three areas of participation: playwriting, acting and appreciation. The spectator had a passive role. It was a theatre of forgetfulness in every sense of the term. The spectator was overburdened by certain fixed prejudices and preconceptions. Social power dominated his individuality which wanted a free expression from all sorts of exploitation, linthinking obeisance to class and caste hierarchy suppressed his intellect and prevented freedom of expression.

The social, cultural and political movements of Kerala from 1920 onwards aimed at developing new means of expression, autonomy and creative participation of the individual in public affairs. Historically speaking, the organized attempt for this kind of expression in theatre can be found in the social revolt expressed in the play, 'Adukkalayilninnu Arangathekku' (From the kitchen on to the stage) by V.T. Bhattathirippad. This is a play or protest against male domination, brahmanical superiority and prejudices, early marriage of young girls to elderly Namboodiris, discrimination of sexes etc. The playwright addressed himself to these issues in a theatrical idiom which made change inevitable. The major plays that followed suit are 'Rithumathi' (Premji), 'Marakkudakkullile Mahanarakam(MRB) etc. Women's liberation, modern education, the need for social involvement, the plight of windows etc have been the themes that inspired these plays. Looking back, one may be surprised to find how scientifically and theatrically these issues were analyzed exhorting the audience to rise in revolt against social and cultural oppressions that appeared in the garb of traditional values. The intentions were to inspire the participants of the theatre movement with a sense of autonomy. The tragedy of modern society is caused by lack of self knowledge and the energy and power to attain it. In these plays the diction and other means of theatrical expression were as progressive as the themes, enlightening the individuals regarding their complex situation in the society. Oppression was a common theme in these works and the purpose and motive was to protest against the causes and circumstances of such slavery.

This kind of protest found a fuller expression in the plays of Thoppil Bhasi especially in his monumental work 'Ningalenne

Communistaki' (You made me a Communist). Here, the issues raised are wider, ranging from economic and social inequality, casteism and feudal prejudices to the establishment of an Egalitarian society. The play was repeatedly produced throughout the country and it is believed to have been instrumental in ushering in the first communist ministry in Kerala (in the world also) in 1957 through a democratic process of free and fair election. Similarly, the protest registered in 'Kanyaka' by Prof. N. Krishna Pillai is equally strong in a cultural and psychological sense. Plays of this calibre are plenty in the language but the influences they have exerted are to be studied separately.

The theatre of protest gathered momentum as years passed when the cultural activists insisted on the people's awareness and their seeing and thinking for themselves. Theatre organizations, with clearly defined political and cultural motives, sprouted in different parts of the state with a firm belief in man's infinite capacity for improvement. What is offered by the authorities is not enough and it must be destroyed or rejected when found intolerable. This process of destruction or rejection can be carried out only after a close scrutiny and deep analysis of the social evils transmitted to the present generation through dictatorial, colonial, feudal and communal agencies over the last several centuries. The revolt represented in theatre was in fact an extension of the revenge and anger felt at the social levels. It was an expression of dissatisfaction and discontentment over the conditions of life in society. The popular theatre was not very much concerned with those problems. It concentrated on cheap entertainment, a combination of music, dance, melodramatic acting and sentimental ideas. There was no provision for serious thinking and analysis of social problems. But the theatre of protest aimed at revolutionary political solution for the latent problems in the society. So every theatre worker had to be politically awake and he had to play a vital role in educating the masses.

The condition required for this theatre of protest was not merely a political awakening. An understanding of the relations between society and theatre was very essential. According to the social activists Indian society is a closed structure, stagnant and retrogressive. It had to be turned upside down to make it effective and receptive to new ideas and challenges. Similarly, the theatre was also overburdened with conventional concepts and ideas. Fresh thinking and understanding was required in the very structure and mode of communication in theatre. Theatre and society had to be mutually supporting and supplementing. One cannot be discussed without a reference to the other. One is actually for and because of the other, not at its expense. Both can have the fullest expression only in terms of this mutual response and co-operation. Thus, theatre is both political and artistic. It should become the best means of cultural communion and communication.

What is expressed above appears to be idealistic. But it was this idealism which spurred at least a small minority of theatre workers on to the production of some serious plays. One such play was 'Nadugaddika' written, directed and produced by K.J. Baby. The playwright has been totally committed to the ideals of social development and audience participation. The play deals with the transfer of power from the British to the Indians and among the Indians, how it is transferred from a new group to another for selfish achievement. This was presented throughout Kerala during 1979-80 and has had repeat performances also. The play projected a hitherto untried technique of the tribals witnessing the transfer of political power. The locale of action is Wynad, the centre of Adivasi culture and their problems. The director seemed to have followed a kind of Brechtian street play pattern. The audience, unlike the elite spectators, became seriously involved with the development of the plot. They were made to doubt, question and answer some of the problems. It was definitely a new way of expressing anger and protest in modern theatre. The innocent life of the tribals with their song and dance attracted the attention of the onlookers. The play brought the simmering resentment out into the open. The protest was so strongly expressed that the play was looked upon with suspicion by the authorities and the players were arrested and no wonder, it became extremely popular because of its deep rooted commitment.

Many similar plays were produced during and after the Emergency. The Emergency declared by Ms. Indira Gandhi unveiled a dark period in the social and cultural life of the country. Freedom of expression and creativity was curtailed and the power syndrome occupied the centre of political administration. The result was an array of frightening incidents secretly reported from different parts of the country with a warning that any one rising in revolt against the authority will be smashed. India proved itself to be heroic and great, developing as sense of rebellion against this undemocratic and dictatorial regime, in Kerala this questioning was to some extent implicit but there were troupes and groups of artists and thinkers who rallied together on this fundamental issue of freedom and survival when ever it was possible. My own play 'Thulsivanam' was written and produced during the period of emergency. When it was staged in Trivandrum as part of the Zonal drama competition of the Kerala Sangeetha Nataka Academy, the Police was all around the Bank Employees Union Hall and I had the bitter experience of being interrogated by an intelligence officer regarding the details of my play. Protest was more powerfully expressed by revolutionary activists like Civics Chandran, K.Venu, Sri. Vasu, K. Sachidanandan and others. A play 'Padayani' was presented by the Wayanad cultural society in the wake of the emergency on the initiative of Idakkadu Muraleedharan, who highlighted the cause of the marginalized and the down-trodden. Madhu Master of Calicut played an important role in propagating the serious ideals and ideas of the theatre of protest. He took initiative in organizir g the play 'Padayani' in different parts of the state. It is one of the early plays in Malayalam which took upon itself the duty of mobilizing the people's power and educating the silent masses on their positive role in social reconstruction. Incidentally, 'Padayani', won the first prize in the state level competition conducted in connection with the Silver Jubilee celebrations of the Kerala Sahithya Parishad, which made it more popular and established it as an example of people's theatre. An important feature of this production was that it demanded a cultural meeting for discussion and protest immediately after the play was produced. It was a successful attempt. Madhu Master's contribution to the theatre of protest in Kerala is all the more valuable when his production of Gorky's 'Mother' is considered. The stage version of the 'Mother' was prepared by him with Maxim Gorky's novel and Bretolt Brecht's adaptation in mind. Hence, it has the qualities of a literary piece as well as effective theatre. The troupe 'Renachethana' presented this play through out the state. In fact, it was one of the pioneering ventures in this category even prior to the 'Nadu Gaddika'.

Most of the activities of the theatre of protest in the state took place in the street. They are generally called Street Plays. It is a strange as well as important theatre experience when one is confronted at a street corner by a committed team of activists presenting a play. This trend has been very active in Kerala. Socially and politically relevant problems like Bus charge hike, privatization of education, communalism, Bhopal gas tragedy, Police atrocities, defection of people's representatives, proliferation of atomic tests, child marriage, dowry system, assault on women, illiteracy, globalization, GHAT agreement, patent rules, environmental pollution etc. were made the subjects of such street plays. The Kerala State Sahithya Parishad, 'Kalajathas' organized by students unions, women's group etc. came forward with strong political statements in an exciting street theatre idiom. Percussion instruments, eloquent rendering, exaggerated gesture, colourful costumes, acrobatics, popular tales, myths and stories were all used to achieve the very specific purpose of attacking the identified social enemies of the people. The folk art forms of the tribals and the villagers were also borrowed when found essential for some musical or dance episodes. The street plays were mostly satirical and humorous thereby attracting the attention of the people in different walks of life. They were accepted as a strong weapon of fighting for a public cause. No wonder that about thirty thousand street plays were performed at different places of India on April 12, 1989 in memory of Safdar Hashmi who was killed by the reactionary forces in the country on January 1, 1989. It is also to be noted that the progressive movements all over the world at one time or another resorted to the call of the street theatre and its aesthetics. 'Agit Prop Theatre', 'Guerilla Theatre', 'Third Theatre', and 'Documentary Theatre' are some of the troupes and movements in different countries which presented street performances effectively. Julian Beck and Judith of Living Theatre (U.S.A.) taught the world how seriously the performance aesthetics can be developed in street plays also. I had the rare privilege of watching their street play in Rome (Italy) in 1980, which protested against capitalism, religious and state intervention in the personal affairs of the people. Irwin Piscator, Brecht and Dario Fo explored the possibilities of this medium to the maximum extent. The Nobel Laureate Dario Fo drew on the Italian popular tradition of the commedia del'arte in many of his plays meant for open-air improvisational performances for informal audiences. I remember with a sense of nostalgia how he hilariously demonstrated his techniques of street performances in a workshop in Rome in which I too was a participant.

Coming back to the Kerala scenario, one must make a special mention of women's theatre experiments in the state. It is of course a recent development. Prof. Sara Joseph, a prominent short story writer has devoted her attention to the women's theatre also S. Sreelatha and Sudhi, graduates of the School of Drama, Trichur, organized a women's troupe 'Abhinetri' in Trivandrum and conducted work shops and play production with gender perspectives. They look at life with a sense of anger, agony and consequently with protest against the interpretations of values through centuries from a 'male point of view'. According to the 'Arthasatra', women are to be fined for attending public performances! Let alone participation in performances. Even today it is not very easy to get actresses for performances because of the irrational male-dominating systems.

The Feminist Theatres also project the injustice meted out to women and their great potential for involvement and participation in the restructuring of society. It is in a way part of the women's liberation movement. There is a women's wing of the Kerala Sastra Sahithya Parishad (KSSP) which scientifically takes up these issues. 'Samatha', 'Manushi' etc. are other organisations working on these lines. Street plays like "Parasupuram Chantha" and "Sita" presented by the women's wing of the KSSP powerfully dramatized with an uncompromising note of protest, the curse of the dowry system nursed and nurtured by a decadent society. It was produced in 1983. In 1989, the same group presented street plays of great vigour and protest embodied in "Njan Sthree", "En Jathi" etc. Other important plays of protest in this category are "Rose Mary Parayanirunathu", "Deva Silakal" etc. "Deva Silakal" produced by S. Sreelatha in which she acted Yasodhara's role, analyzed Prince Sidhartha's selfish motives in denouncing the Kingdom, his wife and son for the sake of enlightenment. All these plays question the authority, the centres of the power and attempt to ask for apology for the denial of fundamental rights to women. C.S. Chandrika, Sajitha and a committed group of women are quite active in voicing the anger and protest so long suppressed in Indian women. It is also to be placed on record that the enthusiasm of the women's theatre groups encouraged the Kerala Sangeetha Nataka Academy to organise an all India Women's Theatre festival at Trichur in 1998.

There are many committed and angry theatre workers and organizations in Kerala. Only a few have been mentioned here. Names like P.M. Antony, P.M. Thaj, Surasu and others can never be set aside in a discussion of theatre of protest in the state because these were brilliant young men who were protest personified. P.M. Antony for instance, was a centre of attack by all the "henchmen" of the state politics and the Christian community for his controversial play "The Sixth Wound of Christ". The whole of the Catholic community in Kerala protested against the play which portrayed a humanized Christ as against the mistified figure adored by the papacy. One of his earlier works, "Spartacus" was equally striking. It highlighted the Greek slavery and connected it with the present. P.M. Thai, in his plays suggestively and symbolically shattered the authoritarian centres while the late Surasu lived an open life of a rebel like his characters who struggled to free themselves from the shackles of conventions and norms. They all wanted a free society and theatre was used as an instrument for the purpose. Another play produced recently in Kerala with powerful undertones of breaking the Icons of power centres is "Ulakutaya Perumal" written by Prof. Omcheri N.N. Pillai. The impotent ruler aspiring to have his successor is the central image of the play. The writer without mincing words quite satirically aims his arrows straight at the controlling men at the helm of affairs who are incapable of delivering goods. Omcheri employs a style of shocking irony, dark comedy and farce in most of his plays. Similarly, an adaptation of Lonesco's Rhinoceros called "Nettikkompan" was produced by Janayana and was applauded by the jubilant audience who could identify with the helpless masses in the play. It was directed by Prem Prasad, a graduate of School of Drama, Trichur.

In short, the theatre of protest as a forum for social enthusiasts has been vibrant in the state for quite a long time. Mostly it is engineered by young artists with leftist inclination. It aims at enlightening the common man and at questioning the so called "upper class and the elite" on contemporary issues directly concerned with peace, food, freedom and social justice, irrespective of caste, creed and sex. Brecht and other innovators have been at the inspiring points. Even Augusto Boal, the Brazilian Theatre Visionary who works for a "Theatre of the Oppressed" is often heard quoted by the well meaning rebellious theatre artists. His protest is registered against the "glossy" proscenium performances and against the misuse of the body, voice, and mind.

References

Wandor, Michelene, Drama Today, Longman Publishing, New York, 1993.

Thomas, C.J., Uyarunna Yavanika. SPCS, Kottayam, 1984.

Pandey, Sudhakar and Tara Porewala, Freya, Contemporary Indian Drama, Prestige Books, New Delhi, 1990.

Benn, Maurice B., The Drama of Revolt, University Press, Cambridge, 1979.

Kershaw, Baz, The politics of Performance, Routledge, London, 1992

Bhattathirippad, V.T., Adukkalayilninnu Arangettekku, D.C. Books, Kottayam, 1994.

Boal, Augusto, Games for Actors and Non-actors, Routledge, London, 1992.

14

Three Perspectives for the Study of Hybridization in the Italian Tango[1]

Enrique Cämara de Landa

INTRODUCTION

As a result of my research into the phenomenon of the acceptance of the Argentine tango in Italy at the beginning of the 20th century, I discovered that a local type of tango has developed all over the country. Today, it's called tango *liscio*, which means "flat". The name *liscio* comprises four couple dances: waltz, polka, mazurka and tango. The tango *liscio* derives from the Rioplatense tango, that was imported from Paris into Italy just before the Great War[2]. Nowadays, the *liscio* is very different from the original tango; even if the presence of the Rioplatense genre has begun to increase again in the last fifteen years, it is a minority urban movement, whereas the *liscio* is very well known in provincial towns and villages all over the country.

In this paper, I will present some ideas concerning hybridization, mainly in the Italian tango. There are two reasons for my choice: first, that I have researched this topic in depth, second, the processes of hybridization are more evident in it. The Rioplatense scene will be mentioned insofar as it helps to understand the questions considered.

Hybridization and Identity in the Tango

Let us consider an example of Italian tango: *Agata*, a satirical song written and composed by Pisano and Cioffi, in the version performed by Nino Taranto. I'd like to point out the contrast between the words of the performer in the introduction ("Adesso ascolteremo un vero tango argentino" "Now we'll heard a true Argentine tango") and the musical and literary traits of the piece, which clearly show the influence of Neapolitan theatrical songs (*canzonetta napoletana di cabaret*). The exotic connotations with which Italian artists and audiences imbued the tango—a tendency that would subject it repeatedly to new processes of hybridization—did not affect the persistence of a symbolic link between tango and Argentine culture. Considering *Agata* is a satirical song, there may be some deliberate irony in these introductory words. Nevertheless, the fact is that during my fieldwork in Italy, I often noticed that people identified the tango with Argentine culture in general. For example, Raoul Casadei (probably the most famous creator and performer of *liscio*, that is, Italian polka, waltz, mazurka and tango) told me that Argentine musicians are unsurpassed when it comes to producing tangos. He also said: "I sometimes enjoy trying to imitate Argentine tango styles, even if I can't reach their level; for example, Piazzolla's."[3]

This identification of the tango with Argentine culture involves a parallel phenomenon in the mind of the majority of Italian people: the unconscious refusal to acknowledge the existence of a kind of tango created in Italy and consumed principally by Italians. This situation is well illustrated in the definition of tango provided by the *Dizionario Enciclopedico Universale della Musica e dei Musicisti*, published by UTET—perhaps the most prestigious music dictionary in Italy today—which discusses Argentine and flamenco tango but, paradoxically, not tango *liscio*. This despite the fact that I have found more than a thousand tangos with Italian lyrics composed in Italy (some of them used in the past, others still performed today or created recently).

In the tango, hybridization is intimately related to the subject of identity. Both appear like *leitmotivs* in the history of this genre (or, if we adopt the expression proposed by the Cuban musicologist Danilo Orozco and apply it to the multitude of "genres" that contain the name tango, as a "generic cómplex"). On example of this "identity crisis"—that sorround tango is the concern of many scholars and amateurs with identifying the title of the first tango (*¿Dame la lata?*, *¿El quecol*, *¿El negro Schicoba?*)[4] and the date of its birth in the Rioplatense area (around 1870's and 80's). Just as revealing is the dismay of such scholars when they find the word "tango" on musical scores published before that period. From 1850's on, this word appeared in *habaneras* written by Zarzuela composers in Spain. Some Argentine composers wrote "habaneras-tango" and the "tango-habaneras", which can be considered part of the transition process leading to the establishment of the Creole tango, as well as the umpteen example of hybridization between similar genres.[5]

The same "identity crisis" occurred in the 1960s, when some "purists" affirmed that Piazzolla's music could not be considered as tango ("This is no tango!" was the criticism most often leveled at Piazzolla's works and in latter periods at other composer's music). This struggle for the definition of the "true tango" continues to be typical of the "orthodox" or traditionalist critics.[6]

During the international dissemination of the Rioplatense tango at the beginning of the twentieth century, the expression "true tango" was present in different languages. Uruguay was always ignored, but the expressions "Le vrai tango argentin", "Il vero tango argentino", "The true. Argentine tango", are to be found in the press and other written documents of the Northern Hemisphere, relating to a wider phenomenon: the transformation of tango when it is received by societies away from its place of birth, something to be considered as a danger by people looking for a single and unchangeable identity for this dance. In this context, it is important to note that the choreographic elements of the tango shocked western society, while its musical elements were almost forgotten due to the controversies caused by the arrival of the new Rioplatense tango).[7]

The choreographic freedom and creativity that marked the beginning of the "original" Rioplatense tango, in addition to the speed with which it spread in the North, resulted in a situation of heterogeneity and confusion. Dance teachers reacted by organizing conferences and publishing handbooks in order to produce a standard code of steps and movements. One of the most zealously pursued objectives of the transformation of tango choreography was to make it more acceptable or decent. These two goals of homogeneity and moral acceptability produced a new style, that gave the users an "illusion of uniformity", but did not avoid the subsequent production of local variants in countries where the tango continued to be danced. Only the English recreational dance schools—that today make up the International Dance Sport Federation—eventually established this "illusion of unicity" in tango choreography through the elaboration of a rigid system of standardized steps, movements, rules of combination and even of costume. The initial process of change was commented in the European press:

> Perhaps, it is not the original tango. What is danced in our country could be an edition....how can I put it?... attenuated....restrained and corrected. There are too many appearance to be saved, too many susceptibilities to be avoided, to enable us to afford the luxury of an 'authentic' tango. Time—big a leveling agent—will perhaps permit the disappearance of so many prejudices and so many... moral concerns.[8]

In Argentina, the perception of this change—which was the consequence of a choreographic hybridization produced by cross-cultural contact—led to the definition of a "original identity" for the tango as well as to its idealized condition of immutability, a quality that appealed to some poets.

"They have changed your face in Europe/they've referred to you in French 'le tango'/but these things have not changed you/and you are still poor like me". From: *Tango, te cambiaron lapinta, that means: Tango, your appearance has been changed*).[9]

Here, the poet anticipates a central issue in the subsequent tango lyrics: gold, that shines in the center of the City (a metaphoric place created by the people born in the suburbs and taking root) causes corruption and a loss of identity. In other words, the hybridizing power that shines in the center of the World—which in that period, for the portenos—threatens to rob the inhabitants of the world's periphery, i.e. the suburbs of Buenos Aires, of their identity.

The poet defends himself against this danger by affirming the tango's impermeability to change, or, to put in other words, the impossibility of hybridization in tango. In view of the continuous and unending hybridization of tango, the persistence in this attitude shown by certain practitioners could be interpreted as a psychological defense in order to integrate the changes into "the nucleus" of the tango identity (with which they identify their own personality).[10]

This tendency towards "identity preservation" that we find in the way different societies produce cultural artifacts, may be explained in part by the dialectics of stability and transformation. The Rioplatense tango originated in a process of hybridization that took place in a rapidly changing society, namely in that of Buenos Aires and Montevideo around the 1880s. If we apply the definition of hybridization (production of hybrid beings) and hybrid (everything that is a product of elements of different nature) to this case, we can explain hybridization on various levels:

— **Ethnic level**: beginning with the discussion of the contribution of the African-South Americans to the tango, and considering that this dance-song genre was born in a society full of immigrants, the majority of which were Spanish and Italian, followed by middle-Europeans, Orientals, Slavs, Syrians, Lebanese, and so on;

— **Sound level**: through the use of the street-barrel organ, flute, harp, strings, piano, guitar, brass band, bandoneon, etc.;

— **Spatial level**: following a line of progressive social promotion through dancing on street corners, *patios de conventillos*,[11] *peringundines*,[12] *academias*,[13] "*casitas*", open air restaurants, theatres, dance-halls, and cabarets;

— **Psychological level of characters**: associated with the genre: the *cafishios*[14], female owners of dance places, *compadritos* and other figures of Rioplatense mythology, who are joined, in every period, by "normal" individuals and groups.

This universe of interactions (that includes a special relationship between oral and written practice) is enriched and complicated when the tango took off in the Northern Hemisphere. Pelinski establishes two kinds of tangos that developed after this process of internationalization: the *porteño* (that is territorialized), and the nomadic (devoted to cross-cultural interactions). This methodological strategy allows him to establish a continuum between "two different ideal types".

The aspect of interaction may be included in the ambroader category of cross-cultural process, and perhaps, it would be useful to try to define the relationships between this important subject—one that has a long history in ethnomusicological research[15]—and hybridization. But, beyond this issues, the debate between "stability"—sometimes confused with "tradition"—and "change" can also be observed in the Rioplatense area. In fact this conflict is so strong in the region that the whole history of the Rioplatense tango is narrated in terms of two opposing tendencies:

— the traditionalist (orthodox), initiated by Francisco Canaro

— The *avant-garde*, which that begins with the innovations of Roberto Firpo, and finds its paradigm in Julio De Caro.[16]

The orthodox school shows a tendency to articulate melodies with rhythmic simplicity; this is the music that is more suitable to popular dancing. The main representatives of this school are Francisco Lomuto, Juan D'Arienzo, Alfredo De Angelis, Mariano Mores, and many others. The avant-garde pays special attention to experimentation with the sound and with the formal structures of tango. Here we find Osvaldo Pugliese, Anibal Troilo, Horacio Salgan, Juan Carlos Cobian, Osvaldo Fresedo, Astor Piazzolla, Dino Saluzzi, Gustavo Mederos, and Juan Jose Mosalini.

I propose to discuss the possibility of considering this dualism as a defense that pursues a kind of "equilibrium between opposing tendencies". Perhaps this criterion could be helpful for explaining both the disruptive force of the conflict between hybridization and identity, and the responses it generates in the behavior of the social actors in the tango.

Triple Perspective about Hybridization

Summarizing the argument to this point, we can say that:

A. The Rioplatense tango was born as a result of a multilevel hybridization process.

B. Its homologous genres also underwent various processes of hybridization. Similar processes occurred in the earlier, contemporary or subsequent stories of Cuban tango and Brazilian tango, among others[17].

C. The cross-cultural diffusion of the tango that took place after the first consolidation process in the Rioplatense area, and its consequences from that moment to the present, can be better understood if we apply the hybridization concept at three levels: of the object, as a process, and as a consideration.

Hybridization in the object

The analysis of the structural traits in the Italian tango reflects, as we'll see, the product of an interaction of the elements (suppression, substitution, transformation, etc.). We have a hybridization case when these elements are of a different nature or come from different sources.

Hybridization as a process

The hybridizing processes in the tango begin with the reception of this Rioplatense genre in Italy and go through consecutive phases, that imply transformations both to the structures—literary, musical, or choreographic—and social agents (individuals, groups, social classes and subcultures). These two kinds of transformations (that can be considered hybridization when the factors are of different nature), are related to changes in the socio-cultural contexts. Thus we can distinguish four stages in the history of the Italian tango.

Reception

The first stage began around 1913 with the arrival of tango in Italy, with a new and daring choreography that was immediately accepted by the upper class. As a reflection of the socio-political situation of that time, the new genre caused different reactions and confrontations between the institutions, such as the church and the government. Newspaper articles of the period, dealing with tango are surprisingly exhaustive, sometimes even obsessive. Many aspects of the socio-political situation of the country are reflected in these articles about the new South-American dance, recently imported from Paris. In this way, tango becomes an excuse for some critics and commentaries that sometimes do not have almost any relation to it. These texts can be classified in the following aspects of hybridization.

Chronological aspect (the various stages in the tango's arrival including date of arrival, sources, characteristics of the source country, etc). The first mention of tango I found in Italian newspapers and magazines dates from 1913, and it becomes a recurring subject immediately afterwards. However, it had been danced in some European capitals some months earlier, Paris being the first city that encouraged the diffusion of tango, as it has done already with other dances, such as the waltz and the polka. In this way, Parisian agencies also acted as mediators between the Rio de la Plata source and the Italian cities, incorporating the tango as another element of the hybridization process. Italians received tango from two different places (Argentina and Paris) and by two different routes: directly through the relationship created by the immigrants (small and horizontal) or through the prestigious influence of Paris news (big and vertical), and indirectly, through the previous reflections in aristocratic and politic London or Berlin media.

Directly: From Argentina (small and horizontal)
From Paris (big and vertical)

Indirectly: Paris—London and Berlin

Some writers evidenced a xenophobic prejudice associated with the South-American origin of tango. Argentina, however close to Italy through its ties to the emigrants, was very far from

Europe and shared different cultural and social values (some of which were inherited from the aborigines). Consequently, in an Italian description of the tango present during a *velorio del angelito*—a ceremony that takes place after the death of a child in the Northern provinces of Argentina—this South-American folk tradition was taken out of context and its real meaning distorted.

The origin of tango was associated with exotic references, from a possible Asiatic origin, to a Cuban, or Spanish one. Some writers recalled that in Argentina the tango was a lower-class phenomenon, still rejected by the establishment (class hybridization).

Choreographic aspects. There are numerous references to the kinetic elements. We had already spoken about the fact that the socially disreputable aspects of tango were associated with its choreography, not its music. There are also references to the appearance of teachers and academies who participated in the hybridization process through their inevitable respective bachgrounds and criteria.

Psychological aspect. Many texts recognize the powerful effect of the tango presented in Italian cities. This effect is manifested in the strong response that it provoked among the Italian bourgeoisie. The sources confirm that the tango's amazing success in the northern hemisphere direclty affected Italian society. It also apparently affected those who had not yet the opportunity for any direct contact with the dance known as the tango and that indicates that the society was affected by something other than a choreographical style or a new diversion. For the European it was treated as an exotic product of mysterious origin, carrying erotic connotations and coming from a marginal social environment. These attributes converted it into an object of curiosity that would be identified with the forbidden. A phenomenon whose sole mention was a transgression and whose continuation promised new pleasures.

Other articles and advertisements from the Italian press related the tango with a color—the "color tango" is mentioned in the descriptions of the dresses worn by upper-class women at high-society balls, with a style and it was even used in shoe advertisements. Prestigious voices belonging to the world of art were also heard; like the voice of Gabriele D'Annunzio proclaiming the virtues of tango: Tommasso Filippo Marinetti wrote a pamphlet in a futurist style against the tango and Parsifal (don't forget that we are in 1913 and this Richard Wagner's Musical drama was being performed everywhere). Italy absorbed every bit of news regarding the tango boom from Paris. For example: the discourse pronounced by Jean Richepin in defence of the tango and his theatre comedy entitled "Le tango"; or "The "Aerial tango", performed in inimitable style by the French pilot Pegoud with acrobatic aerial displays often associated with tango figures.

Local aspects. Milan constitutes a good example to research the type of places in which the new dance was practised: Movies which were not shown in salas exclusively dedicated for projections, but were used in theater rooms especially prepared for this event. It is possible to find references about the choreographic practise of the tango during the intervals between productions. It also mentions the use of tangos together with other dances in the performances of plays, and also productions inspired by the Rioplatense dance (this is the case of the film *Tangomania*, whose production was announced in the Santa Runegunda theater).

Tango was also practiced in the great masquerades held during carnival period, in private dance halls and large clubs. In social circles and societies, dances and formal evening balls were held. The tango could also be found in parties offered in the private homes of the upper class or members of the aristocracy, with newspapers including the inexhaustible lists of personalities that attended the party. The new dance would also appear in fashion shops and its explicit mention and related publicity indicates that it served as a signal to attract an exclusive clientele. Sometimes the instrumentalists and professional dancers that participated in these dance halls are mentioned.

Legal aspects. The tango was subject to official prohibitions and ecclesiastical censurship. We can even find examples of these prohibitions in the Italian press which are motivated by the news arriving from other places, like Berlin, where the Emperor Wilhelm forbad the execution of the dance among his officials; Vienna, where the *Burgmeister* also condemned it, or Paris, where a statement issued by the Archbishop Cardinal Amette (followed by different kinds of reactions in French society, from the formal protests of Parisian dance teachers to anticlerical satirical poems) is reproduced in Italian newspapers.

It is in the ecclesiastical world where the principal condemnation of the tango was verified. It is certain that there were no explicit declarations by the Pope regarding these notions—the story of Pope X and the *furlana* was invented by Jean Carrere, correspondent for *Le Temps*—but there was also the curate of Rome raising his voice against the scandalous novelty. The pastoral letter delivered to the parishes of Rome is followed by a chain of condemnations produced daily by cardinals, archbishops, bishops and colleges of priests. Some of them use the tango theme to point arrows at the layman sector and the progressiveness of Italian society, and this fact is inscribed in the line of attacks that the Vatican sent to the same targets in the moment of tense relations between Church and State. In the Italian Senate a bill was debated about the priority of civil matrimony over religious matrimony and this fact originated daily virulent attacks from both parts, which were published in the press for public commentary.

As a result of such condemnation, some dance teachers began to "clean uo" the choreography of the tango in order to make it "more decent". This explains some of the hybridizing consequences we have already mentioned.

Relational aspects. Besides the *furlana*—which only became fashionable during a brief period of time—other dances are mentioned with relation to the tango on different occasions. The trescone, the *saltarello* and other dances of Italian folklore only appear in the quality of "cousins" or contemporaries of the *furlana*, not as dances in style in Italian cities during those months. On the other hand, the Boston waltz, the one-step, the two-step and other dances are frequently mentioned as fashionable dances, which constitutes reference material about the choreographic practice in Italian halls, and perhaps could have been secondary hybridizatory components in the definition of the local style or performance.

Musical aspects. The music is the great absent figure in the relative documentation at the time the tango was received by the European capitals. Italy does not constitute an exception to the rule. Only three examples of music are found as appendices in the book "Balli di oggi" by Francesco Giovannini. Although the first is well presented as "tango brasiliano", the second as "tango argentino" and the third only "tango", it is not possible to detect the musical differences in these pieces that would allow us to consider them as belonging to a different genres or as significant variants of a genre[18].

Concerning this first period in the history of the Italian tango, I propose the following explanation: local musicians tried to imitate the musical traits of the Rioplatense style, even if they could not avoid minor differences originating from their background seeping into their pieces. In contrast, some dance teachers made changes to their choreography in order to make it "cleaner" and "more decent". Thus, two kinds of hybridizing behaviour can be distinguished: conscious or deliberate (dance teachers), and unconscious or unintentional (composers).

Songs During Fascism

During the First World War, some references—with photo included—about the soldiers dancing the tango in the trenches constitutes the exception to the general silence that fell over all mass-media in regard to the tango and all types of social diversion. Nevertheless, the existence of the prestigious Festival di Piedigrotta—a song competition that took place every year near Naples—would safeguard the continuity of the tango production in Italy (because some artists created and performed tangos in the Festival), and, simultaneously, would produce a hybridizing interaction between the two styles (Neapolitan and Rioplatense).

The second stage took place after the Great War, when the tango was revived with the appearance of the lyrics in the Italian genre (it must be remembered that tango-songs had been created in Argentina in 1917, when Carlos Gardel sang "Mi noche triste"). During these years, more evident differences with the Argentine tango started to arise. Italian tango audiences seem to have preferred the dance from the beginning. When lyrics of the Argentine tango were imported in to Italy, they couldn't understand them and didn't try to translate them. Because of this, a local repertory of sung tangos appeared in the 30s, (which was a very rich time for Italian popular song). Here there is a paradox: from a circumstance of limitation—incomprehension, not translating—a fact of richness was derived (the production of a big repertory that, even having some relationship with the Rioplatense model, reach a consistent degree of autonomy).

The hybrids appear in this period from the beginning: in the film that created a model for the contemporary tango style—Los cuatro jinetes del Apocalipsis (1921)—Rodolfo Valentino, dressed with gaucho clothes, dances a tango in the international style. Local politics are also to be considered: Benito Mussolini liked tangos and applauded Eduardo Bianco's performance when this famous Argentine musician played with his tango group under the invitation of the King Humberto. As a consequence of that, the tango didn't receive the kind of prohibitions suffered by jazz; on the contrary, fascism encouraged the creation and diffusion of local tangos (which formed an extensive repertory). The ambiguity—or contradiction—between the "awareness of property"[19] and the sentiment of dependence on the Argentine led Italian creators of tangos to exaggerate the traits of style that allow the recognition (identification) of the genre. This kind of behaviour transformed some style unities *museme* into cliches. This is particularly evident in the musical formulae: the melodic succession of the dominant-descending V-IV-III scale degrees, that the Rioplatense musicians adopted for the tango[20], was converted into a predictable resource (mainly in particular points of the macro-structure) by Italian tango composers. The accentuation of the arsis in the perfect cadence at the end of the pieces, typical of Rioplatense tango, was used in dynamic, agog and timbre, and exaggerated to such a degree that the final chord of the tonic sometimes disappeared. We should ask ourselves if these cases of exaggeration—which are motivated by the danger of losing the identity of a cultural product when it is imitated—could be included in the hybridization category. Here there is no combination of elements of a different nature or from different origins, but the manipulation of a single element. Perhaps the same phenomenon can be observed when a new element, not belonging to Rioplatense tango, is incorporated into the Italian style. This is the case of the motive break that occurs through the articulation of chords only in uneven pulses (occupying the whole pulse or making its binary division), which gives a sensation of rhythmic stammering and always appears at the same point of the macro-structure (at the beginning of the final chorus).

In other cases the hybridization is obvious: for example, the descending melodic line (from VI to I) followed by a perfect cadence at the end of the theme of Hernando's hide away (which is neither Italian nor Rioplatense) has been taken by Italian composers as a cliche. Perhaps the similarity with the descending line IV-I followed by a lower auxiliary tone, which ends the first musical section of La Cumparsita, could have confounded them.[21]

Among the more evident hybridization that take place in the sound is the combination of instruments used in the Rioplatense area (the guitar, for example), or emblematic of the tango (the bandoneon register in the fisarmonica [22]), with others taken from the local traditions (ornaments used in folk music), or belonging to contemporary jazz bands (trumpet with frequent use of mute, the saxophone)[23] , or typical of that period (vibraphone, cu-cu). Some "neapolitan" tangos include mandolin and two voices singing in parallel thirds. Certain musical themes were used ("Amami Alfredo" from La Traviata, for example), directly quoted or used as models, a vocality stemming from the bel canto style, and a lot of stylistic *museme* (for example: the semantic relationship between descending melodic contours and feelings of sadness, jealous torments and passionate renunciation)[24].

I have outlined some of the changes and hybridization produced in the musical structure. Another change involves the textual structure or the relationship between the musical and literary structure. In this repertory, the text is written over a previously composed melody, so it must match the melodic and rhythmic characteristics. Most Italian words finish on an unaccented syllable, but the final-accented melodic segments caused some adjustments to be made: the first and third person of the preterite and future tenses (*fuggi, sperai, rivedró, tornerai*), the final-accented or monosyllabic adverbs (mai, piu, cost), personal pronouns (*tu, me*), apocopes (*cuor, amor*), etc (Bandini 1996).

Among the "ideational" sources of hybridizations in Italian tango, exoticism is one of the strongest. Phrases like "La pampa infinita me chiede la vida e questa e per te" (the infinite pampa ask me for my life which is for you)[25] or "laggiu nellArizzona/ terra di sogni e di chimere/se una chitarra suona/cantano mille capinere"[26] (there in Arizona/land of dreams and chimeras/if a guitar plays/a thousand swallows sing), indicates that the flat environment of the Argentine pampa can be replaced by the Arizona desert; or the Hungarian *puszta*, where a "gitano dall'aria triste e appassionata" (a sad and passionate gipsy) plays a sweet serenade[27]. And exoticism is what we find in the improbable characters like the Japanese (and obviously abandoned) *Samaka Liù* or behind the frequent confusion between tango and Spanish culture.

Other evidence of hybridization includes (a) the way in which the thematic topics—topoi-of the Rioplatense tango are transformed to conform to the Italian ambience—something we could call "thematic hybridization", (b) the process of "folklorization" or the permanence of some Italian songs in the collective memory of the people to the extreme of forgetting that they were originally tangos (as in the case of *Chitarra romana*), (c) the explicit political allusions (the "fascist" tangos like *Sul lago Tana or Il minatore*), as well as (d) the complex relationship with the local film industry.

Liscio

The third stage is that of the tango *liscio*, which was born after the Second World War. It is an evolution of the previous local tango: some songs are still preserved, but a new homogeneous style begins to spread all over Italy.

The origin of the term *liscio*—that seems to have been applied in Italy after the Second World War—is not well-known, but it probably indicated some special way of dancing in pairs without exaggerating steps and movements[28], like it were used in the Rioplatense tangos after the beginning of the twentieth century[29].

The most widespread hybridizing trait in this repertory is the incorporation of the tango in a tradition developed in various Italian regions—especially in Romagna—from the middle of the nineteenth century: the "bailes de pareja enlazada" (Vega 1956), urban pair dances performed also in rural areas (almost exclusively waltz, polka and mazurka)[30].

In the fifties, the romagnolo[31] musician Secondo Casadei began to incorporate tangos into his repertory. His nephew Raoul Casadei—a "living myth" of the popular music produced in Romagna—followed his initiative, mainly after the new growth of the liscio fashion that took place at the beginning of the seventies. The "Casadei phenomenon" grew so much during those years, that many other musicians decided to adopt his prestigious name for their ensemble, which gave raise to dance orchestras: Giancarlo Casadei, Celestino Casadei, Claudio Casadei, and Ezio Casadei, among others (Manfredi 1981: 29). From that moment on, the leading musical instruments of the *liscio* were the saxophone and the *fisarmonica*, always accompanied by the inevitable rhythm of the slide drum, with the frequent inclusion of the electric bass and the acoustic or electric guitar. Sometimes, other instruments are added to this organological base (which is very different to the standard ensemble used in the previous stage).

Following his commercial instincts, Raoul renewed every aspect of liscio:

— He included new instruments in his ensemble, like the twelve-string guitar[32].

— He composed new pieces (sometimes formal schemes that where different to the usual ones), and incorporated attractive young musicians into his orchestra.

— He created a cooperative and the club *Musica solare*, with a growing number of local branches all over the country.
— He designed and built a big complex—the *Ca del liscio*—that contained enormous ballrooms.
— He founded a musical company—*Simpatia Edizioni Musicali*—exclusively devoted to the publication and distribution of his works (sound and video records, scores, floppy disks).
— He created a radio program—*Navegando col re del ballo italiano*—that was transmitted in more than forty local broadcasting stations.

Today, Raoul continues to increase his activities (related to an agency for contracting shows and organizing musical weekends, travel holidays, and competitions, and to a floating discotheque...). Even if he has tried to renovate the genre creating the "solar tango", he recognizes that his maestro was Castellina, the musician who created a model for the Italian tango. Castellina—whose real name is Roberto Girardi—represents a double stylistic bridge: one between the ambit of traditional music and *liscio*[33], and another between the historical stages[34]. After have operating these two kinds of hybridization—ethnic and historical, Castellina converted the sound that he obtained from his accordion into the defining trait of his performance style; and this is what constituted a model for a generation of Italian tango interpreters. Today, this traditional Italian tango style is one of the most appreciated characteristics of this orchestra[35].

Even though the world of *liscio* is occupied by hundreds of interpreters, the comparison between these two emblematic musicians in sufficient for us to observe the existence of two branches of hybridization—or two "speeds" of hybridization—in the *tango liscio*: Castellina stands for the consciousness of a local tango tradition (forgotten hybridization), whereas Casadei leads the continuous renovation trend that sought to adapt to the changing tastes of young people (renewed hybridization). Castellina's style belongs to a hybridization process that occurred in the past, while Casadei promotes every kind of hybridization in the present.

Castellina: forgotten hybridization (in the past, hidden).

Casadei: renewed hybridization (in the present, obvious).

In Castellina's style the contradiction between an awareness of ownership (of local tango) and the simultaneous negation of it is present once again, because performances of the genre are often announced with the typical: "and now, an Argentine tango!". In the Italian song called "Un tango italiano[36], we have the exception to the rule of contradiction mentioned above: the text is an explicit declaration of identity and identification. Hearing an Italian tango emitted by a jukebox in a foreign country where she lives, the singer—who has been away from her homeland for a long time—recalls her former Italian lover and decides to return to him. The Italian tango melody, that comes to her "between strange sounds of jazz", represents a sign of identity from her past. By identifying with this "home" tango that belongs to her past enculturation process, she finds the way back to her lover, who will no longer be a stranger to her.

Postmodern tango in Italy

The fourth stage in the history of the Italian tango began during the 1980s and is characterized by a continuous—and sometimes strong—hybridization between different kinds of tango styles. The massive emigration of Argentines during the dictatorship of the 1970s, the relationship between cinema and tango, and some very successful shows such as *Tango argentino*, can be considered as some of the facts that produced new approaches to the "original area" of this generic complex. Today in Italy there is a clear coexistence between various types of tango (Rioplatense, *liscio*, Italian song created between the two world wars, standard)[37]; but there are similarities between these styles, caused by social agents that are moved by creative curiosity or commercial interest (such as singer-songwriters, jazz musicians, directives and teachers of the sporting dance clubs). As a result of this, hybridization (viewed as an activity) increases. Old and new sounds can be appreciated living together, folk melodies set to tango rhythms, the use of improvisational techniques in long and asymmetric forms derived from jazz styles, and a strong tendency to integrate and mix different kinds of musical elements.[38] Are these post-modern tangos?[39]

Hybridization as a consideration

The history of Italian tango shows that hybridization can be studied through the observation of the interaction processes between different kinds of traits. This is not to say that these elements are closed, self-sufficient, stables or homogeneous. On the contrary, every component of an hybridizing process can also be seen as an hybrid. Every cultural entity can be analyzed as a trait belonging to a cultural ambit in a particular conjunction of space and time (and this can be done both from outside that culture or from inside it). But the same cultural phenomenon can be considered as a component participating in one or more processes of interaction, that involve both the objects and the people. The Italian tango, for example, can be seen both as a genre belonging to the Italian culture (from outside: we, non Italians, observing it; from inside: Italians composing, performing, hearing or dancing the song called "Tango italiano"); and as a component of interaction processes (in the objects: the relationships between an Italian tango and its Rioplatense model; in the people: the behavior and meanings related to tango in Italy).

In this sense, a melody of tango incorporated in an electronic composition is so hybrid as the tango danced by a couple in a Italian *liscio*-hall. We have historical evidence of this in both cases: in the first case, the interaction between the musical structures, and in the second, the behavior of the people.

The semantic changes (that occurs in every individual mind as a normal part of human perception according to each individual's particular circumstances) are phenomena to be considered in the study of hybridization: The same phenomena can be observed in the semantic explications shared by groups of individuals. An example of this social process can be observed in the opinions of some personalities living in the North Hemisphere about the new arrived tango, published by the magazine *La Nuova Antologia* the 16 January 1914. Their responses cover a wide range of attitudes: rejection, enthusiasm, acceptation and indifference[40]. Although they exhibits a considerable degree of irony, the opinions about tango are related with the considerations, that is, the way everyone looks—or consider—both the new cultural object—the dance—and the growing fashion related with its use.

The objects and processes related to the Italian tango can be considered in different ways: hybridization being only one of them. Applying this particular kind of consideration to a performance of Italian tango, we can observe it as an hybrid *object*, and try to enumerate the traits that confirms this. Or, we can study the hybridizing processes that have led to this consequence. But if we forget the hybridization question and we take into account other tales or possibilities, complementary aspects of the phenomenon under observation will emerge. I quote here only one, related with the significance and meanings involved in the experience of the participants. One of the performers—the dancer Antonello Lanzi, leader of a dance group—wrote to me a letter trying to express his feelings about the tango danced by him and his partner. Let me quote here some paragraphs:

> *Oh, my beautiful Valentino, I've dreamed about dying with you...*, sings a splendid voice with deep performing feeling; and we see on the stage a man and a woman bringing to life the story of the song. They move with sensuality, underling with original figures the music played by the orchestra with mastery an passion. (Personal communication).
>
> The letter reflects Antonello's views of tango as a "danza which figures both give deep feelings, and offer the oportunity to improvise, to communicate, and—above all—for the couple to dialogue through dance" until this ends "with a perfect *casché*", causing the thunderous applause of the public that "awake from a hypnotic trance". Antonello is even more explicit when he writes that "every musical piece has its history, its dialogue, and its language; every couple dance the tango with a degree of skill that is related to their personality and the story they are living". (Personal communication).

Pelinski affirms that "within the objective possibilities related with the musical structures and guided by the vital experience of an audience that is located far from the Rioplatense culture, the nomadic tango can acquire meanings hardly contemplated by the *tango porteño*" (Pelinski 2000: 67). Antonello's testimony offer us an evidence of the complementary situation: a kind of tango that is different from the Rioplatense one, can produce sentiments and sensations that are similar to those originated by the contact of the "original" tango.

Conclusion (Some Questions and one more Example)

I would like to conclude by raising the possibility that the same materials used by scholars to study the Italian tango would allow both to take the hybridization into account and at the same time to ignore it. It might be illuminating to ask how much our knowledge of this tango history would change if we include the "perspective of hybridization" in our research. Today there may be some post-modern tangos in which the presence of the stylistic hybridization principles is even stronger. How often do creators and performers take pleasure in their explicit hybridizing action? Is the value of hybridization growing today?

Final example: During a concert given at the University of Valladolid on August 30, 2001, by *Aires tango*—the Italian complex which style is based on the fusion or tango and jazz music, the leader of the group, Javier Girotto, played some isolated sounds in a *siku* (the andean South-American pan flute), followed by a musical variation over a traditional melody from the North-Western area of Argentina. This use of a folk instrument was an exception in that performance and could be considered an sporadic or isolated hybridization within a context of an explicit hybrid musical style, i.e., a style constructed over a continuous or constitutive hybridization[41]. The same hybridizing attitude that generates a musical style which identity is based on the fusion, temporality produces moments of increased—and even more explicit—hybridization. And these episodes confirm hybridization as a form of identifying behavior for the musical group.

Using a scale of various degrees of hybridization, we could have measured, at that moment, an episode of, say, "the third degree" within the context of a "second degree" style.

Final question: Does the tango possess a specific trait that makes it specially prone to hybridization?

The first possible answer refers to the compatibility of its musical system with others: Following this interpretation, the tango that has always been created by using the grammatical elements and the syntactical rules of the Western tonal system would facilitate hybridizatory interaction with other musics belonging to the same system, more than other based on different systems. The tritonic-system based *baguala* and the pentatonic *huayno* of the South American Andean area, would have less potential for hybridization[42]. Despite this, I have analysed a wide range of hybridatory possibilities between the tonal system and both the tritonic (in the bagualas[43]) and the pentatonic (in the huaynos[44]).

The second possible answer refers to the capacity of interpolation: This is an area that depends on socio-cultural and historical circumstances. During the 1990s, some Argentine rock composers begun to incorporate musical traits from folk and tango, but this tendency could have been motivated by the need to overcome a creative crisis (or by the ability of the musicians) instead of being the consequence of some specific traits of the rock musical system itself. A large dose of caution and hability is necesary for travelling between the analysis of both the objects and the behaviors that produce them, in order to interpret correctly the hybridization process.

Another continuous journey along with the researcher needs to take care, is the methodological movement between the three perspectives of the hybridization phenomenon: the observation of the hybrid object reveals the existence of the hybridizing processes and imply an explicit behavior in considering them. At the same time, the process don't exist independently of the object (people, songs, etc.). Finally, without consideration there is no consciousness of hybridization (that in to say: hybridization simply doesn't exist).

Notes

1. This text is a revised version of the article: "Hybridization in the Tango. Objects, Process, and Considerations", which has been published in Gerhard Steingress (ed.) 2002, *Songs of the Minotaur. Hybridity and Popular Music in the Era of Globalization*, Munster/Hamburg/London, Lit Verlag, pp. 83-112.
2. Rio de la Plata is the region between Uruguay and Argentina in which the tango was born.
3. The Argentine composer Astor Piazzola is well-known everywhere because of his links with tango music.
4. The possibility that *El Queco* could have been the first rioplatense tango or an andalusian one is discussed.. *El Negro* Schicoba could be a piece derived from the candombe (Salas 1986).
5. Al menos hasta que se descubra documentatión todavia inédita, el tema de los primeros tangos se mueve en el piano de las aproximaciones o sencillamente de lo conjetural" (Salas 1986: 52).
6. Pablo Vila (1995) has dealt with the relationship between tango and identity from other point of view: the function played by this genre in the configuration of the ethnic identities of the inmigrants during the twentieth century in Argentina (Europeans in the first stage, Latin Americans, in the second).
7. The European choreography of tango had its own characteristics from the beginning, differing from the Rioplatense. There are reports of a series of movements made by the dancers with rigid precision, something which was really far from the improvisatory principles followed by the Rioplatense dancers of tango during the initial period of its history. We should note that in Italy—as in other European countries—Argentine teachers were more prestigious than the locals. Nevertheless, we must take into account that this European version was born in Paris: "Ma il tango che si balla ora in Europa, confrontato con quello che dalle Antille passo in Argentina, e quasi irriconoscibile. II tango riveduto e corretto ad uso della buona societa e stato inventato a Parigi" (from an Italian newspaper).
8. *Il Teatro Illustrate), anno IX,* No. *XXII,* 15-30 Noviembre 1913.
9. ("Te han cambiado la cam alia en Europa/te han llamado en fiancé s "«le tangó»/pero estas cosas no te han cambiado/y eres todavfa pobre como yo" *Tango, te cambiaron la pinta*).
10. In Psychology the integration is seen as a mechanism of defence that allows the personality to incorporate the changes without losing its identitary nucelus.
11. Buildings inhabited by inmigrants living in poor conditions.

12. Public places for dancing and drinking.
13. Places frequented only by men, in which where possible to pay for dancing with women.
14. Pimps.
15. See the Wachman, Waterman, Ortiz, Nettl and Kartomi contributions; and the application to the nomadic tango by Pelinski (2000).
16. About this stylistic dichotomy, see Ferrer 1960.
17. On this issue see Ortiz & Nunez 1999.
18. For a further description of these tangos, see Camara 1995, 2000.
19. The consciousness about the existence of an Italian tango.
20. This formula, typical counterpoint to the ascendent line from V to I had been used by romantic composers and was very frequent in different popular genres during the thirties (we find it, for example, at the end of the blues scheme).
21. In fact, Gino Stefani (1992: 168) makes this mistake quoting the Italian cliche as the *La Cumparsita* tipical ending formula.
22. The absence of bandoneonists in Italy was compensated by the use of the bandoneon register in the keyboard accordion, that in Italy is called *fisarmònica*.
23. The sound of the jazz bands, forbidden in Italy during Mussolini's rule, appears in the tango that fascistm approved.
24. A more detailed description of the musemes and semantic association in the Italian tango from the Mussolini period, see Camara 1999b.
25. *Munchita.*
26. *Tango delle capinere.*
27. *Violino tzigano.*
28. ...the word *liscio* is not referred to the music, but it indicates the way of dancing it, that requires a continuous *lisciare* [smooth, drag] of the feets" (Chiesa, w/d: 75).
29. "[In the rioplatense towns] the tango coreography suffer a double adjustement. In one hand, it is simplified by the way of dancing "*liso*", that means: without figures." Novatti & Cuello 1980:33.
30. The *galop*, the *cuadrilla* and the *manfrina* were also danced.
31. Born in the italian region of Romagna.
32. "I've crreated the solar *liscio* solar and, consequently, the solar tango. The reason of this term is in its sound. The sounds of violin and clarinet, tipical of the traditional tango, together with the accordion, evoke an open air space where mortadela is eaten. Instead of this, if I include the mediterranean twelve-string guitar and the percussion, I give and idea

of holidays, of the sea, Greece, ships, Sicily, and I encourage turism and international oneness..." (Raoul Casadei, personal comunication).

33. Before he began to compose and perform music to be danced in pairs, he used to play the *organetto*, a bitonic accordion with eight basses and twenty-one melodic stops originating in rural areas.
34. He participated in the multitudinary concerts organized by Mussolini in Rome, playng a *fisarmonica* (that was a gift from the fascist movement).
35. Even if he no longer plays anymore, the young accordionist of his group exhibits the performing style Castellina transmitted to him.
36. Authors: Pallesi—Beretta—Malgoni.
37. During the third stage, the standard dances, based on the rigid codes developed in England by the Arthur Murray School, arrived in Italy, wherer they were a tremendous success everywhere. Italian sport dancers have reached important places in the international ranking and some of them have been awarded first prizes and became famous teachers in their own right.
38. Recently, the ethnomusicologist Tim Rice used an example of rioplatense tango performed in an additive. Bulgarian rhythm to illustrate a paper about "The Attenuation of Bulgarian Nationalism Through Medited Music and Dance Performances" in the 36th World Conference of the ICTM (Rio de Janeiro, July 4-11, 2001).
39. Gerardo Gandini calls "postangos" his performances of well-known Rioplatense tangos.
40. Danza acrobatica, senza grazia, di moda, volgare, 1'espressione materiale del tempo, il risultato di un'esuberanza indisciplinata, sfrenata, focosamente giovanile, decente, dependiente de quien lo baile, risultato naturale delle tendenze della vita moderna, comparableva las sombras del ping-pong, salvaje, atea, demoniaca, reprobable, aburrido, de efectos extraordinarios, disonesto, casto (purche lo si danzi con uno spagnuolo o con un argentino), relajante, antipatico, melancolico, contrario a la sicurezza pubblica" (from an Italian newspaper).
41. Even if most of the audience didn't recognized the folk melody, the use of a *siku* was an evident change. We could say that it was an isolated covert and overt act of hybridization (the hidden melody was played on a visible instrument).
42. "Remember Waterman's theory of affinity, which he uses for proposing that similarities between both southern Sahara's African and European musical systems facilitated the musical acculturation in the Americas (Waterman, 1952).
43. See Cámara "The Baguala" (forthcoming).
44. Cámara 1995.

References

Bandini, F. 1996, "Una lingua poetica di consumo". In Coveri, L (ed.), *Parole in musica. Lingua e poesia nella canzone d'autore italiana*, Novara, Interlinea, pp. 27-35.

Cámara, Enrique 1995, "Procesos de aculturacion relacionados con formas musicales en el carnaval andino argentino de influencia boliviana", Granada, *Cuadernos de Arte de la Universidad*, 26: 297-314.

____., 1996a, "Baguala y proyeccion folklorica". In Jordi Raventos (ed.) Actas del *I Congreso de la Sociedad Iberica de Etnomusicologia (Barcelona, 9-10 de marzo de 1995)*, Barcelona, La ma de guido, pp. 109-143.

____., 1996b, Recepcion del tango en Italia", *TRANS* (*Revista Transcultural de Musica*) 2 (noviembre/diciembre 1996), http://www.sibetrans.es/trans/

____.,1998, "Rasgos musicales de los tangos italianos de entreguerras". In Luis Costa (ed.), *Actas del II Congreso de la Sociedad Iberica de Etnomusicologia (Valladolid, 22-24 de marzo de 1996)*, Santiago de Compostela, Sociedad Iberica de Etnomusicologia, pp. 179-190.

____.,1999a, "Algunas consideraciones sobre el estudio del tango italiano". In Carlos Sanchez Equiza (ed.), *Actas del IV Congreso de la Sociedad Iberica de Etnomusicologia, Granada, 9 al 12 de Julio de 1998*, s/1, Sociedad Iberica de Etnomusicologia, pp. 313-335.

____.,1999b, *Passione Argentina: tanghi italiani degli anni Trenta*, Roma, Discoteca di Stato.—2000(1995), "Escándalos y condenas: el tango llega a Italia". In Pelinski, Ramon (ed.)., *El tango nomade, Ensayos sobre la diaspora del tango*, Buenos Aires, Corregidor, pp. 163-250).

____., "The Baguala: A syncretic vocal expression of Indians, mestizos, and criollos" in Latin American Music". In Kuss, Malena (ed.), *An encyclopedic history of musics from South America, Central America, Mexico, and the Caribbean*, "New York and Farmington Hills, Michigan: Schirmer Books— The Gale Group, 2 volumes.

Chiesa, Riccardo w/d.,"Secondo Casadei: dagli inizi al 1940". In Turci, Mario (ed.), *Il ballo liscio*, Museo degli usi e costumi della gente di Romagna, Quaderno 3, Maggioli editore, pp. 67-77.

Ferrer, Horacio 1960, *El tango, su historiay evolutión*, Buenos Aires, Peña Lillo.

Novatti, Jorge & Cuello, Inés 1980, "Aspectos historico-musicales". In Novatti, Jorge (ed.) *Antologia del tango rioplatense*, Buenos Aires, Instituto Nacional de Musicologia, pp 1-43.

Ortiz Nuevo, José Luis & Núñez, Faustino 1999, *La rabia del placer. El nacimiento cubano del tango y su desembarco en España* (1823-1923), Sevilla: Diputación de Sevilla.

Pelinski, Ramón (ed.) 2000 (1995), El tango nómade, Esnayos sobre la diaspora del tango, Buenos Aires, Corregidor.

Ramón (ed.), *El tango nómade, Ensayos sobre la diáspora del tango*, Buenos Aires, Corregidor.

Salas, Horacio 1986, *El tango*, Buenos Aires, Planeta.

Stefani, Gino 1992, *La melodia*, MIlano, Bompiani.

Vega, Carlos 1956, *El origen de las danzas folklóricas*, Buenos Aires, Ricordi.

Vila, Pablo 2000 (1995), El tango y las identidades etnicas en Argentina". In Pelinski,

Waterman, Richard Alan 1952, "African influence on the music of the Americas", in *Acculturation in the Americas*, Chicago, University of Chicago Press, pp 207-218. [in: Garland Anthology vol 3, Music as culture).

Contributors

S. Murali: Painter, poet and critic—specialist in aesthetics—Professor and Head Department of English, Pondicherry University, Pondicherry.

Ashokamitran: Well-known creative writer in Tamil—has won the Sahitya Akademi award for his novel—widely translated into many languages—also columnist.

Ayyappa Paniker: Highly acclaimed modernist poet and multi-faceted literary critic in Malayalam and English—retired as Professor and Head, Institute of English, University of Kerala—noted for his perceptive and clear-headed thinking.

M. Ramakrishnan: Scholar and critic—Senior Lecturer in Philosophy, Govt. Brennen College, Thalassery, Kerala.

M. Madusudhana Rao: Scholar and teacher—Chairman, PG Board of Studies, Department of English, Nagarjuna University, Guntur.

Usha V.T.: Reader and Coordinator, Centre for Women's Studies, Pondicherry University—authored many noted articles on issues related to women, literature and media

Guillermo Rodriguez Martin is with the Centre for Asian Studies, University of Valladolid, Spain.

B. Chandrika: Better known as Chandramathi—creative writer has won many awards—rated highly as a fiction writer in the Malayalam—with the Department of English, All Saints' College, Trivandrum.

Lalitha Lenin: Well-known poet—advocate for women and dalit voices.

M.G.S. Narayanan: Nationally acclaimed historian and perceptive literary critic–was also the Chairman of the Indian Council for Historical Research (ICHR), New Delhi

R. Raman Nair: Author of innumerable articles and books in the field of library science—currently Librarian in the Govt. Brennan College, Thalassery, Kerala.

Usha Bande is Fellow at the Indian Institute of Advanced Study, Shimla—author of many articles and books on women and fiction.

Vayala Vasudevan Pillai: Well-known drama critic and specialist in theatre—Profesor in the School of Drama, University of Calicut, Kerala.

Enrique Cámara de Landa: Ethnomusicologist from the University of Valladolid, Spain—authored many articles on folk music and theory.